COMMERCIALIZATION OF POSTAL AND DELIVERY SERVICES:

National and International Perspectives

Topics in Regulatory Economics and Policy Series

Michael A. Crew, Editor

Graduate School of Management
Rutgers University
Newark, New Jersey, U.S.A.

Previously published books in the series:

Rowley, C., R. Tollison, and G. Tullock:
Political Economy of Rent-Seeking

Frantz, R.:
X-Efficiency: Theory, Evidence and Applications

Crew, M.:
Deregulation and Diversification of Utilities

Shogren, J.:
The Political Economy of Government Regulation

Hillman, J., and R. Braeutigam:
Price Level Regulation for Diversified Public Utilities

Einhorn, M.:
Price Caps and Incentive Regulation in Telecommunications

Crew, M.:
Competition and the Regulation of Utilities

Crew, M., and P. Kleindorfer:
Competition and Innovation in Postal Services

Thompson, H.:
Regulatory Finance: Financial Foundations of Rate of Return Regulation

Crew, M.:
Economic Innovations in Public Utility Regulation

Crew, M., and P. Kleindorfer:
Regulation and the Nature of Postal and Delivery Services

Oren, S., and S. Smith:
Service Opportunities for Electric Utilities: Creating Differentiated Products

Koble, A.L., W.B. Tye, and S.C. Myers:
Regulatory Risk: Economic Principles and Applications to Natrual Gas Pipelines

Pechman, C.:
Regulating Power: The Economics of Electricity in the Information Age

Gordon, R.L.:
Regulation and Economic Analysis: A Critique over Two Centuries

Blackmon, G.:
Incentive Regulation and the Regulation of Incentives

Crew, M.:
Incentive Regulation for Public Utilities

COMMERCIALIZATION OF POSTAL AND DELIVERY SERVICES: National and International Perspectives

edited by

Michael A. Crew
Graduate School of Management
Rutgers University
Newark, New Jersey, U.S.A.

and

Paul R. Kleindorfer
The Wharton School
University of Pennsylvania
Philadelphia, Pennsylvania, U.S.A.

Kluwer Academic Publishers
Boston/Dordrecht/London

Distributors for North America:
Kluwer Academic Publishers
101 Philip Drive
Assinippi Park
Norwell, Massachusetts 02061 USA

Distributors for all other countries:
Kluwer Academic Publishers Group
Distribution Centre
Post Office Box 322
3300 AH Dordrecht, THE NETHERLANDS

Library of Congress Cataloging-in-Publication Data
Commercialization of postal and delivery services : national and international perspectives / edited by Michael A. Crew and Paul R. Kleindorfer.
p. cm. -- (Topics in regulatory economics and policy series ; 19)
ISBN 0-7923-9514-X (alk. paper)
1. Postal service--Deregulation--Congresses. 2. Postal service--International cooperation--Congresses. I. Crew, Michael A. II. Kleindorfer, Paul R. III. Series: Topics in regulatory economics and policy ; 19.
HE6076.C66 1994
383'.4--dc20 94-36133
CIP

Printed on acid-free paper.

Printed in the United States of America

CONTENTS

AUTHORS AND DISCUSSANTS

John F. Alepa, United States Postal Service
Toru Azumi, IPTP
James I. Campbell, Jr., International Express Carriers Conference
Maurice C. Castro, Australia Post
Robert H. Cohen, U.S. Postal Rate Commission
Jeffrey L. Colvin, U.S. Postal Service
James A. Cotton-Betteridge, Royal Mail International, British Post Office
Helmuth Cremer, Institut D'Economie Industrielle, University of Toulouse
Michael A. Crew, Rutgers University
Nicholas Crew, University of California—Los Angeles
Marc Derycke, La Poste
John R. Dolling, Royal Mail International, British Post Office
Mario Dunn, Union of Communciation Workers
Hans Dydensborg, Price Waterhouse/IKO
Per Forssberg, Sweden Post
André Grimaud, Institut D'Economie Industrielle, University of Toulouse
Thomas Grzesiak, Price Waterhouse
John Haldi, Haldi Associates, Inc.
Frank Heselton, Unites States Postal Service
Ross Hinds, IPC Unipost
Heinz Hofmann, BAPT
Anders Jeansson, Sweden Post
Wynne Jones, Coopers-Lybrand
Paul R. Kleindorfer, University of Pennsylvania
William E. Kovacic, George Mason University
Jan-Erik Leistedt, Sweden Post
Pekka Leskinen, P&T Finland
Maurice Lévy, IREPP
Katsumi Matsuura, Osaka University
Colin J. Mitchell, Eurpean Mail & Express Users Association
Heikki Nikali, Finland Post
Donald O'Hara, U.S. Postal Service
Virpi Palo, Finland Post
John C. Panzar, Northwestern University

Katherine O. Peltier, Price Waterhouse
Mary Perkins, Howard University
Frank Pieper, WIK
Oluf Raldorf, IPC Unipost
Ian M. Reay, Royal Mail
Thomas Reenberg, Price Waterhouse
Paul Richards, European Commission
Alan Robinson, Klick, Kent & Allen, Inc.
Frank Rodriguez, U.K. Post Office
Cathy M. Rogerson, Unites States Postal Service
Roger Sherman, University of Virginia
Walpurga Speckbacher, Deutsche Bundespost Postdienst
Börje Spong, Sweden Post
David Storer, Coopers & Lybrand
Ulrich Stumpf, Frank, WIK
William M. Takis, Price Waterhouse
Junichi Tanikawa, Ministry of Posts and Telecommunications, Postal Bureau
Joëlle Toledano, La Poste
David Treworgy, Price Waterhouse
Hannu Tuominen, Finland Post
Ken Umemura, IPTP
Sture Wallander, Sweden Post
Torsten Zillén, Sweden Post

PREFACE AND ACKNOWLEDGEMENTS

This book arises out of a conference, Conference on Postal and Delivery Services, held in Stockholm, Sweden, May 18-21, 1994, and a workshop, The Workshop in Postal and Delivery Economics held in Hakone, Japan, June 1-4, 1994. Leading practitioners, world-wide postal administrations, and the express industry, as well as a number of regulators, academic economists, and lawyers came together to examine some of the important policy and regulatory issues facing the industry. Issues addressed included international postal policy, including the role of the Universal Postal Union; regulation and terminal dues; competition, entry and the role of scale and scope economies; the nature and role of cost analysis in postal service; productivity; and service standards.

The conference and the book follow our two earlier conferences. In 1990, a conference was held at Coton House, Rugby, England, July 22-25, 1990, in honor of the one hundred and fiftieth anniversary of the Penny Post and the contribution of Sir Rowland Hill. The ensuing book *Competition and Innovation in Postal Services*, was published by Kluwer Academic Publishers in 1991. In 1992, Regulation and the Evolving Nature of Postal and Delivery Services: 1992 and Beyond was held at Village PTT, La Londe les Maures, France, on March 18, 1992. This conference resulted in *Regulation and the Nature of Postal and Delivery Services*, published by Kluwer in 1992. Both conferences were recognized by the European Express Organization with the Hermes Award 1992 at its annual award dinner in Munich on June 22, 1992. The first workshop, The Workshop on Postal and Delivery Economics, was held June 23-26, 1993 in Daun, Germany.

The 1994 conference and workshop were made possible by the support of the following organizations: The Rutgers University, Graduate School of Management, ***Center for Research in Regulated Industries***, The University of Pennsylvania, Wharton School, Center for Risk Management and Decision Processes, Institute for Posts and Telecommunications—Japan, Deutsche Bundespost Postdienst, United Parcel Service, The United States Postal Service, La Poste, The British Post Office, Federal Express, The Swedish Post Office, The United States Postal Rate Commission, Finland Post, Price Waterhouse, the European Commission, New Zealand Post, and Coopers-Lybrand. We would like to thank sponsors not only for financial support but also for their advice and encouragement and for serving on the organizing committee. These include Toru Azumi, James Campbell, Robert Cohen, Frank Heselton, Wynne Jones, Tom Leavey, Kathleen Mullin, Virpi

Palo, Ian Reay, Paul Richards, James Rogers, Cathy Rogerson, Jacques Salais, Marc Smith, Walpurga Speckbacher, Börge Spong, David Storer, William Takis, Elmar Toime, Joëlle Toledano, Sture Wallander, and Anton van der Lande. In addition, we would like to thank Ulf Dahlsten, President and Chief Executive Officer, Sweden Post; Elmar Toime, Chief Executive, New Zealand Post; Yukihide Okano, Director General of IPTP; Robert Cohen, Director—Rates Analysis and Planning; James I. Campbell, Jr., Special Counsel, Postal Affairs, International Express Carriers Conference; and Norimasa Hasegawa, Deputy Director General of Postal Bureau, Ministry of Posts and Telecommunications, Japan. Each, through his after-dinner speech, provided a unique perspective on the problems facing postal and delivery networks.

We would like to thank our hosts for the Conference, Sweden Post, and for the Workshop, IPTP, for help with all of the arrangements and their generous assistance. Finally, we must thank Linda Brennan, Administrative Assistant in the Center for Research in Regulated Industries, for her efforts in making this book possible. In addition, to her usual duties of copy-editing and typesetting, she had the difficult task of collecting the papers. This was no mean task in view of the number and scattered nature of the contributions. We would like to thank her not only as editors but on behalf of the authors too. We would also like to thank Kathleen Rutledge of the Center for Research in Regulated Industries for her valuable assistance with the Conference and Workshop and with the produciton of this volume. The usual disclaimers are applicable. None of the people named here is responsible for any errors. The views expressed are the views of the authors and not of the sponsors.

MICHAEL A. CREW
PAUL R. KLEINDORFER

FOREWORD: THE COMMERCIAL POSTAL BUSINESSES

Elmar Toime

Introduction

My interest in the postal business stems from the fact that it is my livelihood. It's the job that I do. One of my duties is to take an interest in worldwide developments that could affect how the business performs. However, I think the reverse should also be true. I have a duty to explain how the New Zealand Post experience may help the development of the Post around the world.

New Zealand is a small country with a population of some 3.5 million. It is a remote country, and it doesn't matter whether you travel east or west to reach Europe. It is a country that has embarked on a sizable economic reform program. This reform both started and carried on the business restructuring which today makes New Zealand Post highly successful from the standards of either the corporate world or the postal world. These elements—small size, remoteness, and economic reform—are used by many observers to discount the New Zealand Post achievement. It is all very interesting, but it is hardly relevant to what is happening in the real world, they say. I would argue that it is highly relevant. I want to use this opportunity to develop my reasons as to why the New Zealand Post experience is a valid prescription for postal reform, which to me means the same as commercialization. As chief executive of New Zealand Post, I have plenty of reason to reflect on this matter.

It is a fascinating question to ask why the Post is of so much interest. How can there be conferences such as this? Has there been, I wonder, a worldwide conference on fast foods? Perhaps there could be. The theme might be Ramsey pricing based on menu variety! Can you imagine a Green Paper (or should that be a Yellow Paper) on competition in the soap and allied products industry? Surely provision of soap should be a universal service? What is it about the Post? As a practicing and, hopefully, a competitive manager, to see the Post become both profitable and a commercial enterprise is of most concern to me. So, perhaps a little irreverently, we should ask why the Post and its many parts are subject to such analytic interest.

A Point of View

I can illustrate some of the shortfalls of piecemeal analysis by referring to a fascinating book I read on a long plane journey recently. One of the advantages of living so far away in New Zealand is that you get plenty of time to read when you get on a plane! The book is quite captivatingly called *"The man who mistook his wife for a hat"* written by Oliver Sacks, a neurologist dealing with physical disorders of the brain. There is a case history in the book that seems pertinent to this query of mine. The subject, a professor of music, was taken by his wife to see the doctor. There was nothing manifestly wrong; his absent-mindedness was increasing, but otherwise there was nothing you could quite put your finger on.

The interview with the doctor went well, quite normally, except at the conclusion when the professor got up to leave. As he reached out for his hat he seized his wife's head instead, and tried to put it on! He thought his wife was a hat, and hence the title of the book!

Now what has this got to do with deregulation and postal economics and the commercialization of the Post? It seems that the man in the story had an incredible visual disorder. He could see simple shapes and identify them quite clearly and so on, but he could not see the whole. And so we come back to the Post. What is it that the researchers see as they analyze the parts, as they analyze the market, as they evaluate the public interest, as they compute the correct pricing models to use. Do they see the whole business? This is my opportunity to be the good doctor, not the patient.

Commercial Results

What I see when I look at the Post is the whole entity, a normal business, trying to motivate its employees, trying to serve its customers, trying to earn a good rate of return on the investment in its assets. I think our results speak for themselves. New Zealand Post has been a limited liability company since 1987 and has been accounting as such since then, with no special considerations or provisions. In our financial year ending March 31, 1994, we have achieved a 30% return after tax on shareholders funds. We made a $100 million operating profit before tax on a turnover of $620 M—a 16% before tax return on sales.

It is fair to ask how can a monopoly earn those sorts of profits without abusing its market power.

There has been just one price rise in 8 years for the standard letter. (For comparison purposes, that equates to the first-class letter service, a definition we do not use because we have no second-class mail). This was a 5 cents adjustment (a 12.5% increase and tied to our smallest coin) in a period that has seen 30% inflation. When you add to this that we have removed weight steps for letter mail, we believe that we offer our customers very good value. In fact, letter prices for business customers were reduced in December last year, passing back to those customers the benefits of our efficiency. Other significant achievements include:

- We have almost the cheapest letter price in the OECD.
- We've quadrupled the retail outlets where you can buy stamps, but closed three quarters of our Post Offices. On time delivery is better than 97%.
- The workforce has been reduced by 40%, with a 25% increase in volumes over the period. *Real* unit costs, measured by total real expenditure divided by total volumes, have been reduced by over 20%.

What do these results and achievements mean for policy setters around the world? In particular, do these results for New Zealand Post prove that it is a commercial business, and what are the lessons for other postal businesses?

Market Forces

New Zealand Post presently has a limited letter monopoly, a 45 cent letter price against an 80 cent competitive floor price. The existence of this level of protection somehow negates the company's commercial achievements. The combination of high efficiency and low prices cannot persuade everyone that the results are not solely monopoly driven. Market forces, in my view, are the only ones that can answer my question: is New Zealand Post a commercial organization? We need the test of free and open competition to see whether we've got the business formula right.

Before advancing this argument, which in essence is the case for deregulation, it may be useful to distinguish between market behavior and Post behavior. If the distinction is not made, arguments about deregulation will confuse the social obligations which policy setters may judge as necessary with the ideological principle of free competition.

Market behavior deals with the environmental issues of regulation, legal controls on commercial behavior, and competitor freedoms. In a free market economy, it is driven by the belief that consumers are best served when they can choose between competing firms.

Post behavior deals with the policy requirements of governments for services that they may wish a carrier of last resort to provide. That carrier is defined to be the Post. That is the Post's purpose. A totally separate argument deals with the *content* of policy for the social obligations. I will not enter into that debate here. It is not my job. My job is to deliver those policy prescriptions—the so-called social obligations of the Post.

When practitioners and regulators meet, the deregulation debate seems to founder on the question of guaranteeing the social obligations. We must all have a level playing field before competition can take place. Why? If government is prepared to set objectives and meet their cost, the next best thing is to meet them as efficiently as possible.

How to do that? That's where competition and the free market comes in. And if the Post fails and can't cut the pace in that environment? That's when policy setters put their money where their mouth is. They replace the management or they take advice as to how to make ends meet, by abridging some of the social obligations for example. You will never know though until you try. And the cost that will have to be paid will be the true efficient cost of the social obligations.

So, my first conclusion is this. The final test for commercial behavior, that is, efficiency and service, is the ability to survive and then succeed under the pressures of free customer choice. That the Post has additional responsibilities by way of its social obligations is not an argument to deny customer choice. In fact, the benefits of competition may lead to subsequent redefinition of the social obligations. What consumers really want will become much clearer.

As an aside, if this argument is carried, it provides the reason why competitors to the Post should *not* have to have the burden of any social obligations imposed. Why add extra loads to all players? That is re-regulation to my mind. An example of this sort of error is the approach some regulators are adopting of seeking to license all postal operators in a market. It is a market distortion which invites deception by competitors and becomes impossible to police.

The Deregulation Process

The New Zealand Post experience provides a prescription for deregulation, and should be seen as such, rather than as an interesting but not quite relevant case.

Deregulating the Post has several considerations:

- the correct market positioning for the Post;
- defining the social obligations;
- timing for deregulation;
- the real issue: commercial freedom; and
- ownership issues.

These are all meaty subjects, and each no doubt would warrant its own conference.

Market Positioning

The first issue asks what should be the best market positioning for the Post? Consider the four quadrants formed by axes representing competitiveness and efficiency. For simplistic purposes, I will use price as a proxy for competitiveness, so that for example a low price corresponds to high competitiveness. Efficiency is measured by costs, so that high efficiency is the same as low cost.

Quadrant one is the inefficient and low price combination. Here costs are met from *cross-subsidies*, typically from Telecom, where PTT's still exist, or taxation. This model probably covers the developing economies, where valid policy objectives are to overstaff the Post as part of a national employment policy. I have no quarrel with the policy, but I believe ultimately it is wrong. The Post is too important an infrastructure service to allow it to be crippled by inefficiency and unfocused management. But that is not so important as denying the user-pays principle. Whenever a Post loses money then clearly non-users are paying.

The **second quadrant** describes the postal business which is inefficient and covers that inefficiency with high prices. Who will own up to being in that category? This is the most difficult category for a postal manager to be honest

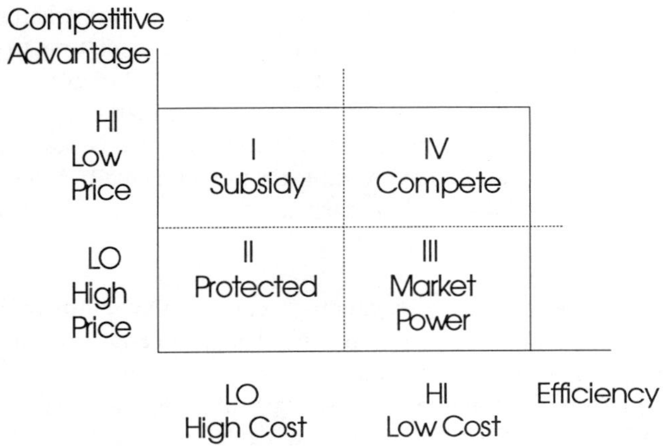

Figure 1. Market Positioning: Price and Efficiency

about? This is where *protection* by regulation is sought after the most eagerly, to hide the need for change.

My third category is the postal business that is efficient but takes a deliberate market stance of using its *market power* to keep prices and margins high. I believe that is a valid market positioning, and, indeed, as a marketer, I see it is a very attractive position to be in. But at the end of the day that is not where New Zealand Post is. Our positioning aim is low cost, low price, the fourth quadrant—the true *competitive* quadrant. As a key infrastructure service in a developed economy, the Post must assist business profitability by keeping prices low. And it doesn't hurt as a position of competitive advantage to be the low cost provider!

So my first consideration in setting out on the path to commercialization is the ability of a Post to decide its market positioning honestly in relation to the efficiency/price mix. International benchmarking helps to evaluate this.

Social Obligations

The second issue on my list deals with the social obligations required of the Post. These are not always as explicit as they should be. They often deal with perceived political realities or lobbies, and hardly ever tested by market research. Nevertheless, perception is reality and these are real requirements of policy setters. The Post, as carrier of last resort, must accept them or, as I insist, must *embrace* them.

In New Zealand Post, these are expressed in the form of a Deed of Understanding with the government, a particularly simple, direct, and practical vehicle which commits the Post to the social obligations. To return to my earlier point though, they define Post behavior, not market behavior.

Transition

In thinking about taking the Post into an open market, the third item on my five point list concerns the element of time. It does take time to restructure the Post. To have a fighting chance, it must be given some time to adapt, time to understand the market and to train its people to think in a different way. Policy setters owe Post people the chance to make their way, because building a marketing presence takes time. The danger though, if too much time is allowed, is that because the Post has to fight to get this recognition that reform takes time, it actually comes to believe its own rhetoric after a while. Reform then stalls.

Communication Behaviors

A fourth consideration for deregulation concerns the future of letter mail. Competition from electronic substitution and changes in communication patterns are possibly the real market issues, not whether the delivery of letters is regulated or not. The postal regulation debate misses this difficulty entirely. It is all to do with how markets are defined. So how does a regulator deal with problems such as the scope of the postal business, or the crowding out the private sector, or questions of constraint of trade which may force the Post to take on an ever-decreasing business role, chasing its tail in ever diminishing circles? Weighty matters indeed.

Well, why should the regulator deal with them at all? There is no reason or incentive to do so. These are matters that concern the protection and development of the investment which already exists in the Post. This investment, whether in capital or know-how or business skills, has been established over a considerable period. It represents real value to the owners of the business. Commercial freedom is the response of the postal manager to protect this valuable asset. It is an issue very different to regulation, and one which requires careful consideration. The separation of regulatory power and executive responsibility, at government, ministerial, and civil service levels is therefore vital. This understanding is of course what is driving postal administration towards the private sector company model.

Ownership

Finally, who should own the Post? Who should carry the risk of commercial success and earn the rewards? If policy setters require activities to be carried out that private sector will not do, then government must devise means to ensure the obligations are carried out. But to provide the rewards and incentives for progress, there has to be more than just running another government department.

So, perhaps there is a case for government to exit the Post. Truly privatize and let the market best meet the needs of consumers and businesses? Commercial freedom would no longer be an issue. It depends on how markets value any such diversification. If shareholders think the value of their equity will increase as a result, then investment in new ventures will be supported. The government as a risk-averse investor cannot make these decisions with the same discipline and unforgiving reaction to wrong choices.

Conclusion

There must always be opportunities to test new assumptions and discuss perceptions of change in core underlying ideas. This conference has a fine record now of running the full range of arguments about how the Post should be treated. Should it be seen as a dynamic but special instance of an industry that must retain the protection it largely still enjoys? Should it be treated no differently than any other dominant business in a market?

I believe deregulation is a policy option whose time has come. There is a way forward and those who will benefit will be those who use the service. The market will prevail! Perhaps one day we will see a conference called "Postal Deregulation: its successes and ....successes." I hope I may be invited to speak at it.

1

A REVIEW OF EFFORTS TO DEVELOP A NEW POLICY FRAMEWORK FOR POSTAL SERVICES IN THE EUROPEAN UNION

James I. Campbell Jr.[1]

Today, the term *postal service* may be taken to refer broadly to any transportation service, public or private, that provides collection, sorting, carriage, and delivery of letters, envelopes, and other small parcels. In virtually all countries, the dominant postal service is the public postal administration or a legal successor with some degree of governmental involvement. In most countries, however, private postal services also offer specialized services, such as mail preparation, express and parcel services, and international mail-forwarding.

For the last six and half years (1988-1994), the European Commission, the secretariat of the European Union[2] has been striving to develop a new policy framework for postal services in Europe. It will soon unveil the product of these labors in the form of a proposed "regulatory framework."

As in other areas of public policy, the multicultural and multinational nature of Europe has led the Europeans to consider general policy problems often neglected by more homogenous societies. Forward-looking and soundly reasoned European legislation would likely serve as the pattern for reform in countries outside of Europe and even for the global postal system, the Universal Postal Union. Regressive legislation will likely have the opposite effect, reinforcing national divisions of commerce in and out of Europe and hindering modernization of large scale delivery services, public and private.

---

1 Special Counsel for Postal Affairs to the International Express Carriers Conference and the European Express Organization. The views expressed in this paper represent the personal views of the author only.

2 The European Union (EU), formerly known as the European Community, consists of the countries of Belgium, Denmark, France, Germany, Greece, Ireland, Italy, Luxembourg, the Netherlands, Portugal, Spain, and the United Kingdom. The supreme legislative authority in the EU is the European Council, a committee consisting of the heads of government of all Member States. The permanent secretariat of the EU is the European Commission.

Almost all of this great European debate appears in government documents and working papers inaccessible to the general reader. For those outside the fray, this chapter attempts to recount briefly the efforts of the European Commission to devise a new policy framework for European postal services.

1. Brief History of Postal Policy

In order to understand any regulatory reform proposal, it is necessary to appreciate the origin, purpose, and development of the regulatory scheme to be reformed. No serious student of public policy would advocate the regulation or deregulation of telecommunications or aviation industries without ascertaining the purpose of the current regime and the manner in which changing economic and technological factors may have eroded original premises. In postal policy, however, the extreme age of basic concepts is often allowed to obscure the need to begin at the beginning.

The original idea of a "postal" system was a series of "posts" or relay stations, housing men and horses. Postal systems were established to provide rapid transportation for correspondence and documents. A walking or riding messenger would travel from one post to the next, handing off the "mail" or pouch to the next messenger. Postal systems are as old as, and probably a necessary attribute of, large scale civilization. Extensive postal systems were developed by the ancient Persians, Romans, and Chinese. These, however, were generally reserved for the use of the government and military; they had little or no direct influence on the development of modern postal systems.

The roots of current postal systems date from thirteenth-century Europe. In this period, the revival of commerce outpaced the reconstruction of large scale government. Between the thirteenth and fifteenth centuries, groups of merchants, universities, and monasteries reinvented the ancient idea of postal systems and developed their own international postal routes.

Between the fifteenth and seventeenth centuries, the French and English crowns incorporated the private postal systems into the government posts and prohibited new private systems. Exclusive control of the posts proved useful as a source of money and political favor and as a means of controlling the plots of rivals for the throne.

In 1840, the expansion of commerce spurred by the Industrial Revolution led England to adopt a thorough revision of the concept of postal service. Series of posts were replaced by railroad and steamship lines. The fundamental function of the postal system shifted from *transporting* mail between post offices located in different cities to *collection and delivery* of letters sent to individual offices and homes, more often than not within the same city. Within a few years, the British Post Office stopped being an expensive service suitable only for the wealthy and the extraordinary; it became a *universal service* suited to the communication of all manner of ordinary commercial and personal messages. The English model was soon adopted worldwide.[3]

Development of universal governmental postal service in the mid-nineteenth century increased the demand for international as well as domestic postal service. Since national postal monopolies had cut off evolution of international postal systems, a second-best solution was adopted. In 1874, national postal monopolies agreed to a standard set of rules for exchanging international mail under the supervision of a permanent inter-governmental organization, the Universal Postal Union.

In the late twentieth century, the appearance of inexpensive long-distance telecommunications and air transportation gave rise to a new generation of private postal systems. These private posts thrived where governmental posts were weakest. They specialized in especially rapid and reliable transmission of letters and documents between cities and across national boundaries, and thus, between national postal monopolies. In essence, the new private posts unwittingly reinvented, at a global level, the concept of private international posts pioneered by Italian and French merchants and universities in the thirteenth century. The new private posts soon came into conflict with the national postal monopolies which had been enacted to control their spiritual forbearers.

At the same time, increasing use of computers has blurred distinctions which were fundamental to the nineteenth-century policy framework for postal services. Computers can print thousands of similar transactions with individualized information (such as statements of account) in a process more akin to printing than individual correspondence. Computers can also produce printed and bulk letter mail in sequences sorted for postal delivery, sharply reducing the cost of postal processing. Computerized databases of customer preferences greatly enhance the effectiveness of advertising by mail. In sum, these developments have called into question the presumption that a single universal postal service for letters can meet the basic needs of society.

At the international level, the evolution of multinational companies has also undercut the premise that international postal service can be organized as an exchange of mail between national markets, each reserved for a national post office. Today, it is unclear which national post office can lay claim to the international mail of a large company with operations in many countries. On the other hand, it is quite clear that a large company can escape a too restrictive national postal monopoly by generating and posting its international mail in another country.

---

3 The seminal paper making the case for reform in England was written by Rowland Hill in 1837. In the United States, postage rates were lowered and the monopoly strengthened in 1845. The United States adopted most of the other English reforms in 1863, with the introduction of "free city delivery." In China, the extensive government post was opened to private citizens in the fifteenth century. Sophisticated private posts also developed in parallel. Postal development in Japan followed a similar course, although later in time. In the second half of the nineteenth century, China and Japan adopted the European model, transforming their postal systems into universal delivery systems provided by a single government monopoly.

Postal administrations have responded to these developments with a mixture of conservatism and innovation. Resorting to postal monopoly laws and the market allocation provisions of the UPU Convention, postal administrations have waged long legal and political battles to block the rise of private postal systems and the transfer of international mail between countries. At the same time, postal administrations have introduced an ever growing array of new services and tariff structures designed to meet the changing needs of users and limit the inroads of competitors.

By 1988, no major government had adopted a new vision of the postal services sector comparable to the English revolution in 1840, but several partial solutions had been tried. Beginning in about 1970, governments began to give post offices greater freedom to introduce new services and respond to the market without truly eliminating governmental involvement in commercial operations. Express services were excepted from the postal monopoly, but the underlying justification for the monopoly was left unexamined. In United States, Congress gave the post office greater commercial freedom but also required it to submit to regulation by an independent agency. The U.S. Postal Rate Commission was established to review new postal rates to ensure that a undue fraction of fixed costs is not borne by customers captured by the postal monopoly. Postal customers and competitors were given full access to this process. While the resulting rate structure is considered broadly fair by all parties, the establishment of the Postal Rate Commission has left untouched the most fundamental problems of the U.S. Postal Service.[4]

2. Chronology of the Commission's Work

With this historical tapestry as background, the European Commission began, in late 1988, a comprehensive review of public policy towards postal services in Europe. The immediate stimulus for this review was the postal administrations' concern with increasing competition from international private express companies. Postal attempts to suppress competitive entry into Europe had been foiled by European competition laws and intervention by the European Commission. When the express companies began services that competed more directly with traditional international airmail services and sought legal protection for these as well,[5] the

4 The Postal Rate Commission, for example, has no influence on the total revenues collected by the U.S. Postal Service. Nor does it regulate the quality of postal services provided.

5 The private express companies began to offer "remail" service, whereby a large mailer in Country **A** could post his international airmail in Country **B**, for delivery in **B** or forwarding to third countries. This practice undercut the postal monopoly over outward international mail in Country **A**. In 1987, the major European and non-European post offices devised a counter strategy that involved higher charges between post offices for the delivery of international mail (terminal dues), interception of mail not posted with the mailer's home post office, and improved business services. In July 1988, the private express companies formally complained to the European Commission that some of these practices violated the competition rules of the Treaty of Rome.

postal administrations appealed to the Commission to undertake a broad review of the purposes and requirements of universal postal service.

The Commission's initial survey of the postal services market took almost four years and resulted, in June 1992, in a 361-page report called the *Green Paper on the Development of the Single Market for Postal Services* ("*Green Paper*"). The *Green Paper* set out a factual and economic description of the Community's postal sector and a proposed policy framework for the Community. The *Green Paper* precipitated a wide-ranging public debate on the future of postal policy in Europe.

During the following year, the Commission received more than two hundred written comments on the Green Paper. Commenters included Member State governments, commercial users and consumer groups, postal and private operators, and management consultants. The Commission also organized and consulted a group of senior officials from Member State governments called the Senior Officials Group on Posts (SOGP). A compilation of all written comments on the *Green Paper* was published by the Commission. In June 1993, results of this consultation and proposed next steps were summarized in a communication from the Commission to the European Council called the *Guidelines for the Development of Community Postal Services* (*"Guidelines*").

In December 1993, the European Council instructed the Commission to draft a proposed legislative framework. In mid-1994, the Telecommunications Directorate (DG XIII) released a document, *Proposal for a Regulatory Framework for Postal Services in the EU* (*Proposed Framework*), which apparently indicates the direction of still unannounced legislation.[6]

In addition to the economic considerations identified in the *Green Paper*, the Commission's analysis has been influenced by two external factors: law and politics. The Treaty of Rome is the constitutional treaty uniting twelve Member States into the European Union. It provides generally that the European Union shall comprise an area "in which the free movement of goods, persons, services and capital is ensured." The competition rules of the Treaty prohibit, in particular, agreements between undertakings or actions by dominant undertakings that may result in the "prevention, restriction or distortion of competition" in "trade between Member States." A public monopoly, such as a postal monopoly, may be tolerated only if full application of the competition rules would render fulfillment of a specific public interest operationally impossible, not merely more difficult or more complicated. Even this slim exception is unavailable if it would prove "contrary to the interests of the Community." The Treaty thus appeared to constrain the Commission's options, at least at the cross-border level.

The politics are more complicated. Postal administrations are among the largest commercial organizations in Europe; in 1988, they employed about 1.2 million persons and earned revenues of around $29 billion ($26 billion ECU).[7] The

6 Although this document has been released by DG XIII, it has not been approved by the full European Commission and could be revised before approval.

majority of European postal administrations fear competition and have urged the Commission not to reduce the scope of the postal monopolies or the legal duties which are said to justify the monopolies. Different administrations have participated in the postal policy debate to different degrees,[8] however, and with different messages; the Dutch Post Office, in particular, has urged liberalization of the monopoly and greater flexibility in legal obligations. Business mailers purchase about 80 percent of postal services and favor greater competition among public and private postal services, especially for the distribution of cross-border mail and bulk mail. Private postal services generally favored greater competition as well. A third political element was presented by consumer groups, whose concern is not so much the existence or absence of a postal monopoly as a desire for a governmental guarantee of a minimal level of universal postal services.

Over the course of this six-year policy gestation, the public debate has centered on three major themes. The first two are *universal service* and the *postal monopoly*, the fundamental concepts imbedded into the idea of postal service during prior centuries. Should the Community ensure a universal service? What should this universal service include? To what extent should the Community accept national postal monopolies, now referred to as "reserved areas"? What role should the new private international postal services play in the commercial development of Europe? The increasingly mixed public/private nature of the postal services sector has added a third theme: *regulation*. Should an independent regulator supervise the conduct of that market? By what standards? We shall consider the treatment of each of these themes through the several stages of policy development.

3. Universal Service

The first recommendation of the *Green Paper* was that the Community should define and guarantee a "universal service" that would be available throughout the Community.

> A reference definition should be decided for the universal service to be applied throughout the Community. This definition will need to take into account the Community's social and economic requirements. . . .[9]

The universal service would include collection, transport, and delivery of a range of letters, printed papers, and small parcels up to a certain weight limit, apparently 2 kilograms.

---

7 *Green Paper*, ch. 4 § 4, p. 74; id., ch. 6 § 3.1, p. 151.

8 Some sense of the activity and contributions of the various postal administrations to the European debate may be gleaned from the number of pages taken in the comments in *Liste*: France (15), Germany (16), Ireland (77), Italy (4), Luxembourg (3), Netherlands (13), Spain (8), United Kingdom (79). The postal administrations of Belgium, Denmark, Greece, and Portugal did not submit comments.

9 *Green Paper*, ch. 9 § 1.1, p. 241.

The *Green Paper* also alluded to a narrower, more fundamental concept of universal service, a universal service for *letters*.

> Universal provision could be required of different types of service (or different uses made of services). These different types of service will naturally have an order of priority in terms of the importance of ensuring that they are safeguarded. In this regard, the fundamental imperative is that universal service must be ensured for postal communication items of a personal or individualized nature....[10]

The postal reforms of 1840 had resulted in postage rates for letters that were uniform throughout England, and the practice of uniform national postage rates had been adopted by most European postal administrations. Nonetheless, the Green Paper specifically eschewed the uniform national tariff as an element of the Community's universal service guarantee or as a justification for a postal monopoly. Instead, the *Green Paper* proposed that the Community assure universal service at *affordable* postage rates.

In the consultation after publication of the *Green Paper*, virtually no major group disagreed with the abstract proposition that the Community should guarantee the availability of some level of postal service for Community citizens living throughout Europe. Substantial disagreements appeared, however, over the nature and level of service to be guaranteed.

Business users expressed skepticism of a broad universal service definition, citing two major concerns. First, they questioned whether a homogenous, governmentally decreed standard would meet the needs of users. Second, they worried that an expansive universal service definition could be used to justify an inflated postal monopoly. The Union of Industrial and Employers' Confederations of Europe (UNICE) commented:

> The *Green Paper* does not examine whether the notion of "basic universal service" really corresponds to a market need. It goes no further than affirming the need for it without giving a precise definition. This affirmation should not be used as an alibi, either for the maintenance of extensive reserved services or to justify existing and/or new cross-subsidization practices between reserved and non-reserved services.[11]

The most commercially minded of the European post offices, the Dutch Post, went so far as to question the continued vitality of the traditional concept of universal service:

> The interests and needs of users and their circumstances have changed so much that it is impossible to cater to everybody by means of more or less identical services. Universality wrapped up as uniformity gives the public postal organizations too little latitude in the marketplace. It creates friction

---

10 *Green Paper, ch. 8 § 3.1, p. 186.*

11 1 *Liste* § 7.2, UNICE, p. 3.

> because the users themselves expect the suppliers of services to be increasingly customer-driven and flexible.[12]

The U.K. Post Office also opposed a broad universal service definition. It argued a universal service area that is greater than the reserved area could constrain a postal administration from competing with private operators on unequal terms. For a postal administration, services which fall within the universal service area but outside the reserved area could be hamstrung by legal and regulatory requirements not borne by unregulated private competitors. The U.K. Post Office's conclusion was that the reserved area and the universal service area should be more or less coterminous. The private operators substantially agreed.[13]

Most postal administrations, however, agreed with the *Green Paper* and supported a universal service definition broader than the reserved area, including postal items weighing up to at least two kilograms. Consumers' groups and some postal administrations went further, urging that the universal service guarantee be extended to include the delivery of parcels as well as letters.

As noted above, the *Green Paper* declined to enshrine uniform national postal rates into the definition of universal service. Instead, it proposed universal service should be cast in terms of *affordable* universal service. Commenters on the *Green Paper* generally failed to recognize the economic significance of the Commission's approach. A postal administration which is able to vary postage rates within reasonable limits is much better equipped to deal with competition and hence much less in need of legal protection from competition. Even if they missed the economic significance, however, commenters evinced little support for mandatory uniform tariffs. Business groups and consumers generally endorsed "affordable tariffs" as the proper standard.[14] The Dutch Post Office maintained that reliability of service, rather than the uniform tariff structure, should be regarded as the key element of universal service.[15] The U.K. Post Office noted the uniform tariff was not mandated by United Kingdom policy, but "it is its preferred position."[16] The French post office observed only that the uniform postage is "currently the case."[17]

One of the more economically sophisticated commenters, the German research group Wissenschaftliches Institut für Kommunikationsdienste (WIK), argued that,

---

12 2 *Liste* § 8.1, PTT Nederland, p. 1.

13 2 *Liste* § 8.1, U.K. Post Office, p. 14.

14 The European level business and consumer groups generally endorsed "affordable" tariffs without further elaboration. The British Institute of Directors questioned the need for a uniform tariff guarantee even within the reserved area. 1 *Liste* § 7.2, Institute of Directors, p. 5. The U.K. Consumers Association supported the uniform tariff principle, but weakly. In a poll of United Kingdom consumers, none of whom have ever experienced a non uniform tariff, one-third rated maintaining the uniform tariff as "unimportant." Of the two-thirds who said the uniform tariff was "important," only four percent rated it as the "most important" feature of postal service. 1 *Liste* § 7.1, Consumers Association, p. 28.

15 2 *Liste* § 8.1, PTT Nederland, p. 3.

16 2 *Liste* § 8.1, U.K. Post Office, p. 43.

17 2 *Liste* § 8.1, La Poste, p. 2.

for a postal administration, the introduction of geographic rate variations for large business mailers is the best way to minimize circumvention of the reserved area without lowering the uniform tariff for individual mailers below cost.

> If a postal administration is obliged to offer a geographically uniform tariff and if such a tariff necessitates cross-subsidization of rural areas, the administration can become vulnerable to cream-skimming. . . . Large volume posters should be allowed to geographically differentiate tariffs for large volume [mailings] (large business customers, private operators posting non-reserved mail).[18]

The point of guaranteeing affordable "universal service" is to protect affordable service to rural areas; few believe that, absent a Community guarantee, delivery services will suddenly disappear from cities and towns. Nonetheless, the *Green Paper* did not explicitly address standards for rural service.[19] Some commenters, however, emphasized the economic importance of this issue. WIK suggested that specific service standards for rural service was one of the most important matters left unfinished by the *Green Paper* but does not offer any suggestions as to how rural service standards might be derived.[20] The private operators group, European Express Organization (EEO), proposed universal service standards for rural areas "should be reasonably related to service standards in the nearest urban areas so as to prevent a sense of isolation or remoteness." Similarly, suggested EEO, the notion of "affordable" universal service in rural areas could be defined as a postage that is reasonably related to, but not necessarily identical to, the rates available in urban areas.[21] While few postal administrations commented on service standards for rural areas, the Dutch Post Office, emphasized that the standard of universal service to rural areas must be flexible because, "holding on to uniformity in defining universal service leads to disproportionately high costs, in other words to macro-economic wastage and the tendency to maintain large postal monopolies." [22] A British poll suggested substantial flexibility in the expectations of consumers regarding rural service.[23]

---

18 2 *Liste* § 11, WIK, p. 13.

19 In his original proposals for reforming the British Post Office, Rowland Hill suggested that postal policy permit price and service distinctions between urban ("primary") and rural ("secondary") areas. A prominent economist, Professor R.H. Coase, commented with the benefit of a century's hindsight:
"There is indeed good reason to deplore the abandonment of the distinction between primary and secondary distribution. It . . . might have led to a rational discussion of price policy and its relation to costs. As it is, the magic word 'uniformity' has been substituted for thought."

20 2 *Liste* § 11, WIK, pp. 2-3.

21 2 *Liste* § 8.2, European Express Organization, pp. 38-41.

22 2 *Liste* § 8.1, PTT Nederland, pp. 2-3.

23 The survey asked about service modifications that might be necessary to keep down costs or adjust to competition. About half of those who live in rural hamlets or villages, or in detached houses, stated that they would accept the introduction of mailing boxes at the end of drives or gardens. 1 *Liste* § 7.1, Consumers Association, p. 4. This seems a high figure considering that

In summarizing the consultation for the European Council, the Commission's *Guidelines* stated that:

> Most contributors felt that the definition of universal service should be broad and should apply to all mail (some mentioned a 2 kg weight limit). The universal service should be based on a uniform structure of reasonable prices and a universal network. Opinions were divided on the sending of goods by post (parcel post).[24]

In an appendix, however, the Guidelines noted that the consultation did reveal a basic philosophical disagreement about the scope of items that should be covered by a universal service definition.

> On the one hand, there are those who support the idea of an extensive universal service and propose extending this definition to all correspondence (a 2 kg limit would seem acceptable). . . .
>
> On the other hand, there are those who would prefer a more limited definition and suggest the universal services apply essentially to correspondence between individuals, although this could also include the mailing requirements of small businesses.[25]

After thus summarizing the consultation, the Guidelines proposed that universal service be defined to include all letters and packets weighing less than 2 kilograms and all parcels weighing up to 20 kilograms.

The *Proposed Framework* maintains a universal service guarantee covering the collection, transport and delivery of newspapers and periodicals, addressed mail items weighing up to 2 kilograms and addressed postal parcels up to 20 kilograms. In addition, the *Proposed Framework* proposes to include a number of specialized services in the universal service definition: special delivery services, recorded delivery and insured service.

4. Postal Monopoly

The *Green Paper* endorsed the proposition that "in order to ensure universal service at a price affordable to all, a set of reserved services must be established."[26] The *Green Paper* envisioned the postal monopoly, or "reserved area," as an economic advantage for the public operator proportional to the obligations of universal service. That is, revenues from the reserved area are not intended to support the entire postal network, only to give the public operator enough of an economic boost so that it can assure provision of universal services, some of which would be provided in competition with private operators. In the view of the *Green Paper*, the

---

door-to-door delivery has long been provided by the U.K. Post Office as a matter of course.

24 *Guidelines, § ¶ 2.2.1, p. 6.*

25 *Guidelines, Annex 2, § ¶ 3.2.1, p. 10.*

26 *Green Paper*, ch. 9 § 1.1, p. 241.

reserved area would thus be as small as possible consistent with the provision of universal service. The *Green Paper* made clear that, in general terms, it believed that such an approach to reserved services is mandated by the principles of the Treaty of Rome.

Based upon this "principle of proportionality," the *Green Paper* proposed that the postal monopoly should exclude goods, publications, or express services, since such services were generally outside the postal monopoly already and hence demonstrably unnecessary to support universal service. In addition, the *Green Paper* proposed that the Community should place upper bounds on the weight of postal items and the price of postal services that could be included within the reserved area. It suggested the price limit for the monopoly should be one and half to two times the postage rate for a letter of the maximum weight that could be reserved. The maximum weight, in turn, "should almost certainly be less than 500 grams."[27]

In addition, the *Green Paper* proposed two other specific limitations to the monopoly: liberalization of cross-border mail and direct mail. Liberalization of cross-border mail was justified, concluded the *Green Paper*, because:

- The cross-border services of the public postal operators are significantly worse than national services and hence competition by private operators promises to improve Community level service, eliminating a "border effect" and unifying the Community economy.[28]
- Cross-border services are already substantially competitive in fact.[29]
- Competition will give users greater choice.[30]

The *Green Paper*'s proposal to liberalize "direct mail" reflected its conclusion that the postal monopoly should be limited to the carriage of "letters." The essence of a "letter" was found to be a communication prepared for a specific person.

> The essential point is that the text in the communication should relate to the business or personal affairs of the addressee (either an individual, an organization or a position within an organization) with sufficient individuality that it is clear that the text (excluding the address and any appellation) refers specifically to the addressee.[31]

The Commission observed that all Member States reserved the carriage of letters. As far as printed papers were concerned, however, the Commission found the situation unsatisfactory:

> The view of most Member States is that printed publications should be in the non-reserved area. However, the regulatory view on direct mail is rather different. More than half the Member States seem to consider such mail as

27 *Green Paper*, ch. 8 § 10.2, p. 208.
28 *Green Paper*, ch. 8, § 8.1, p. 195. *See also Green Paper*, Annex 15 §§ 3.2-3.3, pp. 355-56.
29 *Green Paper*, Annex 15 § 3.1, p. 355.
30 *Green Paper*, Annex 15 § 3.6, p. 357.
31 *Green Paper*, ch. 9 § 9.1.2, p. 201.

> reserved. Part of the reason is that, for at least three Member States, no distinction is drawn between letters and direct mail.[32]

A further complication was that "direct mail" was defined differently in different Member States. The confusion arose because, with modern computers, printed papers such as direct mail could be "personalized" for each addressee and thus qualified as "letters" under the laws of some Member States and not others.

The *Green Paper* proposed to resolve this uncertain boundary to the postal monopoly by looking to the most fundamental social purpose of the monopoly, which was to ensure the universal service delivery of individualized communications:

> Proposals for the regulatory position of printed papers should be formulated by reference to the basic principles of the universal service provision. The absolutely fundamental policy imperative is that postal communications of a personal or individualized nature should be collected and delivered universally. Such mail would include all items where the text is not identical, and would therefore include all personal correspondence and individualized business correspondence. . . It seems appropriate that the set of reserved services that would be established to safeguard the universal service should be based on such items of an individualized nature.[33]

On this basis, the *Green Paper* proposed that all non-letters should be considered outside the monopoly. This rule would exclude parcels and printed publications, which were outside the monopoly anyway in most Member States, and it would exclude direct mail, even of the personalized variety. Other sorts of computer-generated bulk mail, such as invoices and statements of accounts, would be retained within the letter monopoly because their essential message is individualized.

The *Green Paper* recognized that direct mail constituted a substantial fraction of all mail and that sudden liberalization might create difficulties. It therefore proposed further study of the possible problems.

> In summary, there are strong arguments for placing direct mail in the nonreserved sector. However, it should be recognized that there could be difficulties. Firstly, the increasingly personalized nature of direct mail gives rise to growing difficulty in distinguishing direct mail from ordinary letters. Secondly, direct mail presently generates a significant, and rapidly growing, proportion of postal administrations' total business, and its economic relevance to the universal service obligation should be analyzed in detail.[34]

Two other postal monopoly reforms proposed in the *Green Paper* were of considerable importance. The *Green Paper* proposed liberalization of *document*

---

32 *Green Paper*, ch. 7 § 4.1.2, p. 173. Moreover, the Commission concluded that the "regulatory view" was not always indicative of commercial reality. The monopoly as enforced may be smaller than the monopoly on paper.

33 *Green Paper*, ch. 9 § 9.1.3, p. 202.

34 *Green Paper*, ch. 9 § 9.1.3, p. 203.

exchanges. A document exchange is a system of offices where companies which communicate frequently with one another can drop off and pick up letters. To provide long distance services, letters can be shifted from office to office within the document exchange before collection by the addressee. The *Green Paper* also proposed liberalization of *mail preparation*, that is, the collecting and sorting of mail, and possibly the transportation of the mail to the post office that will actually deliver it. Liberalizing mail preparation would permit small and medium sized companies to consolidate their mail using third party contractors, thereby obtaining the same bulk discount rates as the largest mailers.

In general, business groups and the private express companies applauded the *Green Paper*'s proposals to limit the postal monopoly. Postal administrations, with the exception of the Dutch Post Office, opposed. Consumers' groups, whose focus was the availability of service rather than the means of financing it, did not participate extensively in the debate over postal monopoly issues.

In endorsing the need for a reserved area and relying upon the principle of proportionality as the ultimate test for the scope of reserved services, the *Green Paper* rested heavily upon the proposition that there is a discoverable economic relationship between the quality or scope of universal service and the existence or extent of reserved services. Indeed, the *Green Paper* declares, "Universal service without any conditions about price can be provided in the competitive (non-reserved) sector."[35] However, suggests the *Green Paper*, to reduce unaffordable free market prices to affordable levels, a postal administration needs a reserved area to achieve either greater economies of scale and scope or higher profits on less costly mail than it could otherwise obtain in a competitive market. What, then, is the economic relationship between universal service and reserved service?

A number of commenters questioned whether there is any demonstrable relationship between a reserved area and a given level of universal service. The European Express Organization argued that even if a postal administration provides some portion of the universal service at a loss,

> there is no clear reason why the loss must be paid by means of cross subsidy hidden within the accounts of a postal monopolist. . . . At bottom, the postal monopoly is a mechanism for raising money to pay for certain public policies. Any other source of revenue would serve as well, and almost any other source of revenue would be less restrictive than a nation wide monopoly over a class of delivery services, the great majority of which would be produced competitively if permitted.[36]

The Dutch Post Office suggests that a reserved area may have a *negative effect* on the supply of universal service.[37]

35 *Green Paper*, ch. 9 § 1, p. 241.

36 2 *Liste* § 8.2, European Express Organization ¶ 124.

37 The EEO also offered calculations to show that, under reasonable assumptions, plausible changes in the volume of mail will not significantly affect the affordability of postal tariffs. 2

> The first material reality is that monopolies (extensive in some member states) have not achieved the objective for which they were granted. The Green Paper makes explicit mention of the frequent absence of efficient and reliable services, especially in international mail. Similarly, the monopolies in force in almost all member states have failed to produce postal services with a financial balance between income and expenditure. Yet the Green Paper says a reserved sector is necessary, to attain these objectives. . . .
>
> The member states with the heaviest losses are often those with the largest monopolies. So, exactly the opposite standpoint would seem to be the right one. There are also member states with very small monopolies who more or less break even or obtain a normal return by providing good quality services. In other words, the achievement of a financial balance depends on entirely different factors.[38]

The U.K. Post Office pointed out, "There is no conclusive evidence on which to establish with confidence the extent of competition which is compatible with a guaranteed provision of a universal service at an affordable price.[39] Nonetheless, the U.K. Post Office argued that a reserved area is necessary to permit universal service *at a uniform tariff*, that is, to prevent selective competition where the uniform rate substantially exceeds actual costs.[40]

The weight and price limits to the postal monopoly proposed in the *Green Paper* elicited a mixed response. Major business groups, private express groups, and the Dutch Post Office agreed with the concept of weight and price limits; they either agreed with the Commission's proposed figures or offered alternatives. Most postal administrations supported a postal monopoly over items weighing up to 1 kilogram. The U.K. Post Office opposed liberalization of cross-border and direct mail but supported more stringent weight and price limits than proposed by the *Green Paper*: a weight limit of 200 grams and a price of $0.73 (50 pence).

Major business groups supported the *Green Paper*'s proposal to liberalize cross-border mail. For example, the U.K. Institute of Directors, echoing the *Green Paper*'s concerns about cross-border service quality, stated

> Cross-border and international mail is the aspect of postal service which appears to be least satisfactory under present arrangements, and where competition between NPAs and other operators might enable the very improvements in services which would help bring about the desirable

---

Liste § 8.2, EEO ¶¶ 126-136. The EEO's calculations are not based upon actual postal cost data, but they appear to be consistent with studies by the U.K. Post Office that suggest the loss of even large amounts of mail to private operators will not have a drastic effect on the affordability of postal service. For example, according to a United Kingdom postal study, the loss of 50 percent of local traffic in cities outside of London would apparently cause only an 8 to 10 percent increase in the overall price of postal service (public and private). 2 *Liste* § 8.1, U.K. Post Office, p. 51.

38 2 *Liste* § 8.1, PTT Nederland, p. 5.

39 2 *Liste* § 8.1, U.K. Post Office, p. 26.

40 2 *Liste* § 8.1, U.K. Post Office, p. 49.

> economic and social goals identified in the *Green Paper*. . . . The IOD believes that *such mail should be non-reserved*, as suggested in the *Green Paper*, but also believes that stronger controls are necessary to prevent the unfair protection of NPAs.[41]

The Dutch Post Office likewise supported liberalization of cross-border mail, arguing forcefully that liberalization was required for sound commercial reasons.

> PTT Post BV fully endorses the deregulation proposals contained in the Green Paper and the reasoning advanced by the European Commission. We believe deregulation should be introduced as soon as practicable.
>
> In practice, the problem is beginning to center around the situation where it is impossible for the public postal organization of the country of sending to offer customers a reliable service for which it can accept responsibility. Given this situation, it is understandable that business users who depend on reliability decide to use private carriers.
>
> When one considers the present abominable quality, it is difficult to take seriously the call by some member states to keep this cross-border mail in the reserved sector. The postal laws of the member states have never formulated the monopoly on this mail as a specific and explicit objective. Neither do the UPU regulations contain any arrangements for this matter.
>
> Keeping cross-border mail outside the reserved sector will accelerate the improvement of quality and provide a fresh boost for the postal industry as a whole. As well as traffic growth, it will create new opportunities for service-providing companies to spread their wings within the EEC or beyond. Viewed from this angle, the deregulation proposal would make the market more efficient, more dynamic and more versatile. Viewed from the other angle, it is largely indefensible in legal terms to keep cross-border mail in the reserved sector. The number one consideration, however, is that the entire gamut of users want deregulation because they consider the monopoly to be unjust and a restriction of their freedom of choice.[42]

Except for the Dutch Post Office, however, postal administrations opposed liberalization of the cross-border postal services. Their argument was essentially that the provision of universal service requires a reserved area and that any significant reduction in the scope of the reserved area would endanger universal service. Liberalizing cross-border would reduce the scope of the reserved area and was therefore inconsistent with the *Green Paper*'s primary goal of maintaining universal service.

As the consultation proceeded, postal administrations abandoned the argument that competition in the carriage of cross-border mail, only a few percent of all mail, would endanger the provision of universal service. They focused more on the argument that modern mail production technology would permit private cross-bor-

---

41 1 *Liste* § 7.2, Institute of Directors, p. 2.

42 2 *Liste* § 8.1, PTT Nederland, p. 8.

der services to compete with *domestic* postal services. For example, the statements of accounts of a bank located in Member State **A** could be printed in Member State **B** and transported back into Member State **A** for delivery by private postal services. The postal administrations did not explain how cross-border service could improve upon local postal service for local mail. The U.K. Post Office argued that the threat was not so much from superior service but from lower prices. If a post office maintains a uniform national tariff, it earns a extra profit on urban postal services in order to cross subsidize losses in rural areas. A cross-border postal service delivering bulk domestic mail could concentrate on mail to urban and thus "skim the cream" from the domestic mail market. The private operators countered that this argument depended entirely upon a quantitative demonstration of how much "cream" there was to skim as well as an explanation as to why postal administrations could not introduce more cost-based, non-uniform tariffs for bulk domestic mailers. It was noted that the *Green Paper* specifically rejected the proposition that merely maintaining the uniform tariff was a justification for a postal monopoly.[43]

The possible use of modern computer and telecommunications technology to shift production of mail from one Member State to another was also reflected in the proposal by some postal administrations that *outward* cross-border postal services could be liberalized while retaining the postal monopoly on *inward* delivery. If a business mailer in Member State **A** can easily produce his cross-border mail in Member State **B**, there is no reason for a postal administration to insist upon a monopoly over the outward dispatch of mail since it will be impossible to extract monopoly rents from such a service. In any case, many postal administrations recognized that there are few economies of scale associated with the collection and transport phases of postal service.[44]

The major parties followed a similar, but not quite identical, path in addressing the *Green Paper*'s proposal that direct mail should, *a priori*, be considered outside the reserved area. The business mailers generally favored liberalization of direct mail. The group most directly affected, however, the Fédération Européene du Direct Marketing (FEDIM), was undecided whether to agree with liberalization of direct mail or press for liberalization of all bulk mail; some FEDIM members were concerned that treating printed commercial mail differently from other bulk mail might stigmatize it as "junk mail." Private operators agreed on the merits of the *Green Paper* proposal, although they displayed ambivalence over the political wisdom of immediately liberalizing such a large chunk of the postal market.

The strongest arguments in favor of the *Green Paper* proposal were made by some business mailers and by the Dutch Post Office, which contended that a monopoly over direct mail had been rendered unduly burdensome by changing technology.

---

43 *Green Paper*, ch. 8 § 3.2, p. 187.

44 Tabor, p. 36, in Crew and Kleindorfer (1991).

> As well as direct mail, there is a wide range of other means of communication for distributing advertising, so there are ample alternatives. Therefore it would be incorrect and unwise to place direct mail in the reserved sector.[45]

Other postal administrations opposed liberalization of direct mail as a threat to the reserved area that sustains universal service and, in particular, a threat to the maintenance of a uniform tariff.[46]

In the general debate, other reforms to the postal monopoly proposed in the *Green Paper* were largely overshadowed by the attention spent on these major issues. The majority of postal administrations opposed *Green Paper* proposals to liberalize document exchanges and mail preparation. The French Post Office, however, broached the idea of liberalizing mail preparation services——i.e., the collection and transport of mail——as an alternative to liberalization of cross-border and direct mail. The private operators, naturally, supported the *Green Paper* proposals.

In the *Guidelines*, the Commission reported a consensus on the need to maintain reserved services:

> nearly all contributors considered that a set of reserved services should be maintained provided these included only what is necessary to provide the universal service in accordance with the principle of proportionality.[47]

With respect to the scope of the reserved services, the *Guidelines* stated that there was disagreement on the appropriate weight and price limits and that "most contributors" considered that direct mail should be kept in the reserved sector. In regard to the proposed liberalization of cross-border, the Commission noted that "a considerable number of contributors" distinguished between outward and inward cross-border services. Liberalization of outward services was said to be favored by many commenters, while some postal administrations opposed. On liberalization of inward cross-border services, the *Guidelines* reported,

> Most operators opposed liberalization of this stage of the cross- border mail service, chiefly because of the risk of national mail being routed through other countries; most of the companies using the cross-border postal service and private operators mentioned the poor quality of the service and emphasized the advantages of the same operator being responsible for the service from beginning to end.[48]

The *Guidelines* then set out the proposed approach of the Commission. The *Guidelines* confirmed the Commission's intention to propose specific weight and price limits for the reserved area, but gave no specifics. It suggested, as well, that a Member State might not have to abide by these limits if it "felt the specific

---

45 2 *Liste* § 8.1, PTT Nederland, pp. 6-7.
46 2 *Liste* § 8.1, Platform of German and French Post Offices, p. 3.
47 *Guidelines*, § 2.3.1, p. 7.
48 *Guidelines*, § 2.3.2, p. 9.

liberalization proposals could prevent it from achieving the objective of providing a universal service." In regard to the proposed liberalization of cross-border mail, the *Guidelines* called for further study.

> The Commission considers that liberalization of the collection and carriage of outward and transit traffic would not cause serious difficulties.... However, the Commission takes the view that it is advisable to continue to study the implications of liberalizing the delivery of inward traffic and its financial impact, taking into account that this liberalization would bring improvement in performance quality through a single end to end service, in order to reply to the preoccupations expressed during the consultation about the possible diversion of national mail.[49]

With respect to liberalization of direct mail, the Commission stated that it "has noted the problems identified during the consultation but considers that they are not in the long term insurmountable." The Commission recommended continued study of this proposal as well.

The *Guidelines* also suggested a wholly new approach towards the postal monopoly deserved study: the preservation of a monopoly on final delivery of mail while liberalizing upstream operations (collection, transport, sorting), with no distinction between domestic and cross-border mail. The approach was said to exhibit a number of apparent advantages such as guaranteeing the financial viability of postal administrations, compatibility with "the logic" of the Single Market, and controlling the problem of diverting domestic mail into a liberalizing market.

The *Proposed Framework* begins by speaking of "the lasting guarantee of the supply of the universal service, justifying the retention of exclusive or special rights in favor of universal service suppliers." The *Proposed Framework* confirms that the Commission's intention to set weight and price limits on the reserved area but omits specific figures. Unlike the *Guidelines*, the *Proposed Framework* makes no mention of a Member State being able to exceed these limits. The *Proposed Framework* declares that document exchanges should be considered outside the reserved area but defines the term "document exchange" restrictively to prevent the interconnection of document exchange offices.[50] Liberalization of mail preparation services would be limited because the reserved area could include "roadside collection" and transport of mail. Outward cross-border services, however, would be declared outside the reserved area.

With respect to the two major liberalization proposals of the *Green Paper*, the *Proposed Framework* makes an opaque statement that:

> The elements needed to justify the settings of direct mail and incoming cross-border mail in the reserved area are not evident and it should be noted that the answers given [by postal administrations] are not sufficiently

49 *Guidelines*, § 2.3.2, p. 10.

50 In the United Kingdom, the interconnection of document exchange offices has been permitted since 1981.

> convincing in this regard. In this context, delegations are asked to comment on this perspective, giving justifications for their views.

The *Proposed Framework* also confirms the Commission's intention to study the option of limiting reservation to the area of final mail delivery.

5. Regulation of Postal Services

In the course of studying the postal services sector, the Commission gradually concluded that some form of independent regulator is necessary to oversee the provision of monopolized postal services and police the boundary between the monopolized and competitive postal service markets. Of the three cardinal points of the *Green Paper*, however, regulation was the least well developed and the least well critiqued during the consultation.

For the *Green Paper*, the starting point in considering the topic of regulation was the principle that commercial and regulatory functions should be strictly separated. To this end, the *Green Paper* proposed that each Member State should establish an impartial regulator to oversee the scope of the reserved area (i.e., to enforce the "principle of proportionality") and the provision of universal service by the beneficiary of the reserved area. The *Green Paper* emphasized that the regulator must be impartial towards all operators and towards users and consumers.

> In order to achieve this impartiality, it is essential that the regulatory body be separated from any operational function [so that] all concerned (the consumers, the reserved service provider(s) and the private operators) are all convinced of the regulatory body's impartiality. . . .[51]

The *Green Paper* envisioned that regulation should involve oversight of the universal services, not merely reserved services. As noted above, the reserved service was viewed as a subset of the universal services, one that generates sufficient profits to cover losses encountered in reserved and competitive universal services. For the *Green Paper*, the universal service definition thus delineated the jurisdiction of the regulator.

The *Green Paper* gave little guidance on the procedures for regulation but repeatedly relied upon transparency—"vigorously transparent treatment" at one point—as a necessary ingredient of regulation. Thus, the *Green Paper* called for transparency (public disclosure) of access conditions and costs, preferential postage rates, subsidies and cross-subsidies, service targets, and actual service levels achieved.[52]

According to the *Green Paper*, regulation would be directed to ensuring that certain principles would be observed in the supply of universal services:

---

51 *Green Paper*, ch. 8 § 12.4, p. 212.

52 *Green Paper*, ch. 9, §§ 4.8, 6.2 6.6, 5.5, and 8.1, respectively.

- all persons should have access to similar universal services under similar conditions;
- tariffs for universal services should be related to costs, including the tariffs postal administrations charge for the delivery of cross-border mail; and
- quality of service standards should be set and the actual quality of service monitored.

The second of these purposes, relating prices to costs, led the *Green Paper* into the economic complexities of *cross-subsidy*. The *Green Paper* proposed that cross-subsidies from reserved services to competitive services should generally be prohibited. However, it also proposed major exceptions to this rule. A cross-subsidy would be permitted to maintain a uniform tariff or to sustain a universal service, where such cross-subsidy is "compatible with the competition rules." This latter limitation is unclear since almost all cross-subsidies would seem to be incompatible with the competition rules. The *Green Paper* proposed that any price below "average cost" would be considered the object of a cross-subsidy.

With respect to cross-border postal services, the *Green Paper* declared that postal administrations should charge each other for the delivery of mail the same basic prices that they charged their own citizens for the delivery of similar domestic mail. Traditionally, these charges, called *terminal dues*, were set by the Universal Postal Convention and bore no relation to the domestic postage rates. Under Article 25 of the Universal Postal Convention, postal administrations are authorized to refuse delivery of mail that is not posted with the mailer's national post office. Recourse to Article 25 protected postal administrations against circumvention of the uneconomic terminal dues system and effectively allocated the international postal market among the national postal administrations. The *Green Paper* declared that application of Article 25 to intra-Community mail was incompatible with the Treaty of Rome and indeed, that application to external mail could only be justified if invoked by an independent regulator. In keeping with the principle of separation of commercial and regulatory functions, the *Green Paper* also suggested the European Union should have a greater voice in the activities of the Universal Postal Union.

During the 1992-93 consultation, there was unanimous support for the abstract principle of independent regulation of postal services offered by the postal administrations. Business mailers, consumers, and private operators stressed the importance of the regulators' independence and transparency of regulation. As UNICE declared,

> UNICE considers that transparency in the costs of reserved services is a priority. Such transparency is essential to prevent any cross-subsidization from reserved to competitive services.[53]

53 1 *Liste* § 7.2, UNICE, p. 5.

These groups also generally supported the principles of equal access to postal services and the establishment and monitoring of quality of service standards. Although unmentioned in the *Green Paper*, the consultation revealed a consensus among business users and consumers that a postal administration should be required to provide some form of redress for services, at least reserved services, which failed to meet minimum standards set by the regulator.

Aside from the British and Irish post offices, postal administrations offered little comment on regulatory issues beyond broad support for the principle of independent regulation. The British and Irish post offices generally drew a distinction between regulation of reserved services and regulation of universal services outside the reserved area. In respect to reserved services, their position was generally supportive of the regulatory principles espoused by the *Green Paper*, although the U.K. Post Office objected to transparency for postal costs. For universal services offered on a competitive basis, these post offices argued that strict regulation and transparency of prices and costs would unfairly restrict their ability to compete. The European Express Organization agreed with these post offices on the importance of limiting detailed regulation to reserved services, although EEO also pointed to the need to subject other competitive services jointly produced with monopoly services to sufficient control to enforce prohibitions against cross-subsidy of competitive services with revenues from reserved services.[54]

The regulatory issue which provoked the most comment was cross-subsidy of revenues from reserved services to competitive universal services. The major user groups, business and consumer, all objected to the *Green Paper*'s suggestion that funds from reserved services should be used to cross-subsidize competitive services. UNICE's dictum that "The setting of rates for reserved postal services must be based on the principle of cost recovery, avoiding all cross-subsidies to free services" parallels the U.K. Consumers Association's demand that "there is no public interest justification for the subsidy of non-reserved services from profits made on reserved services."[55] These views were also supported by the private operators and at least one post office, the U.K. Post Office.[56] Other major postal administrations, however, supported the possibility of cross-subsidies from the reserved area to support universal services.[57]

Among the more technical comments, there was also broad agreement that the *Green Paper* erred in proposing average cost as the definition of cross-subsidy. The WIK, European Express Organization, and U.K. Post Office suggested that a less stringent test was appropriate, *viz.*, that postage rates should be deemed free of cross-subsidy if they covered marginal costs plus some additional amount that

54 2 *Liste* § 8.1, U.K. Post Office, p. 14; id, An Post, p. 63; 2 *Liste* § 8.2, EEO ¶ 232.
55 1 *Liste* § 7.2, UNICE, p. 5; 1 *Liste* § 7.1, Consumers Association, p. 10.
56 2 *Liste* § 8.2, EEO ¶ 239; id., § 8.1, U.K. Post Office, p. 39.
57 2 *Liste* § 8.1, Platform of German and French Post Offices, p. 2.

reflected either the demand for the service or, more generally, a fair contribution towards fixed costs.[58]

Business mailers, private operators, and the Dutch Post Office agreed with the Commission's proposals to base terminal dues on domestic postage and greater EU involvement in the UPU. Among other postal administrations, some agreed in principle, but argued that reform of terminal dues should be delayed until a consensus could be reached at the worldwide (UPU) level before application within the EU. A number of postal administrations argued that any such reforms must be accompanied by long transition periods. There was little support among postal administrations for terminating their ability to invoke Article 25 or greater Community involvement in the governmental aspects of the Universal Postal Union.

In the *Guidelines*, the Commission reported unanimous support for the principle of independent regulation and declared that separation of the regulatory powers from the operational functions "should be broadened and deepened." The Commission observed that a number of different opinions had been put forward on the subject of cross-subsidy, and proposed that "cross-subsidies from the reserved sector would be authorized if they proved necessary to provide a universal service and were compatible with the competition rules." The *Guidelines* also called for "transparent accounting." While noting that opinions were divided on the establishment of detailed services standards for universal services outside the reserved area, the *Guidelines* proposed to establish service standards for all universal services. Standards for national services were to be established by national regulators and standards for cross-border service were to be established at Community level.

In regard to the alignment of postage rates for cross-border mail (terminal dues) and domestic postage, the *Guidelines* declared that the consultation had revealed substantial agreement with the principles advocated in the *Green Paper*. The *Guidelines* then stated that

> The Commission takes the view that it is not for the Community to take any prime action in this area, which is essentially the responsibility of the operators.

Without mentioning Article 25 of the Universal Postal Convention or a Community role in the UPU, the *Guidelines* called for "compatibility between the international commitments entered into by Member States and Community legislation and policies" and agreed that "ways must be bound and implemented" to prevent the remailing of intra Community mail through external post offices and back into the Community.

The *Proposed Framework* requires that "the regulatory function must be ensured by an entity independent from public or private companies offering services in the postal sector." The *Proposed Framework* maintains the position in the *Guidelines*

---

58 2 *Liste* § 8.1, U.K. Post Office, p. 69; id., § 8.2, EEO ¶ 240; id., § 11, WIK, 20.

that all universal services, not only reserved services, should be subject to regulation, but the principles to be enforced are reduced to general phrases: universality, equality, neutrality, confidentiality, continuity, and adaptability. The *Proposed Framework* makes no mention of transparency for prices or costs of postal services. It states only that the results of quality of service monitoring should be published at least once per year.

The *Proposed Framework* does not define the term "cross-subsidy." It states, however, that cross-subsidies will be allowed from the reserved area to competitive universal services.

> The cross-subsidies from the reserved to the non-reserved area are only permitted when they are proved necessary for the universal service. In all cases, the competition rules will have to be followed.

The *Proposed Framework* makes no mention of a Community role in the governmental aspects of the Universal Postal Union.

6. Summary and Conclusions

In the *Green Paper*, the European Commission made a serious effort to address the fundamental principles of postal policy and reconcile centuries-old precepts with the needs of a modern, multi-country region and the requirements of the Treaty of Rome. The *Green Paper* proposed to retain the nineteenth-century imperative of a broadly defined universal service, but to render it more flexible with the standard of affordable tariffs, rather than uniform tariffs. It proposed to allow maintenance of the national postal monopolies but to place upper price and weight limits on the postal monopolies, thus permitting private express services.

Most importantly, the *Green Paper* proposed four key liberalizations to the postal monopoly. Liberalizing direct mail would confine the postal monopolies to their original content, the transmission of individualized letters. Allowing private postal services to again offer the cross-border services which the national postal monopolies are least well equipped to provide would facilitate development of the Single Market. Placing mail preparation outside the monopoly would stimulate new possibilities for computerized mail sorting and processing. Liberalizing document exchanges would facilitate communications between subsets of users with particularly frequent communications needs. To render the remaining national postal monopolies more accountable, the *Green Paper* also proposed clearly defined standards of service and transparency, enforced by an independent regulator.

Publication of the *Green Paper* generated an informed and illuminating public debate. The consultation revealed a broad consensus among business mailers (who account for about 80 percent of mail), private postal operators, consultants, and at least one post office (the Dutch). This group generally favored the liberalizing proposals of the *Green Paper*, offering economic, commercial, and legal considerations to support their views. However, they disagreed with the *Green Paper*'s broad definition of universal service and advocated a narrower and more flexible definition of universal service, tighter restrictions on cross-subsidy from the reserved area to the unreserved area, and stronger (but perhaps more narrowly drawn) regulation. Consumers favored a broad definition of universal service as well as strong regulation. Most postal administrations supported the *Green Paper*'s broad definition of universal service, opposed any significant reduction of the postal monopoly, opposed transparency of costs, and advocated the right to subsidize competitive universal services from postal monopoly revenues. On key points, however, the postal administrations failed to produce quantitative data to support contentions about the deleterious effects of the *Green Paper*'s liberalization proposals.

If analysis of postal policy proved difficult, political resolution has turned out to be almost impossible. In the *Proposed Framework*, as it now appears, the European Commission will withdraw essentially all of the reform proposals set out in the *Green Paper*. In so doing, the Commission has offered no economic or legal evidence that would contradict the thrust of its previous analysis. Instead, the Commission appears to making an unprincipled political decision to support the interests of the majority of postal administrations rather than the interests of the major users and private operators. However, to the extent that this may indeed be the thrust of the final legislation (which is unclear), it seems certain that such an approach will not resolve the current postal policy debate in Europe. The *Proposed Framework* fails to address important legal considerations which will now be taken to the European Court of Justice by users and private operators. Nor does the *Proposed Framework* address the needs of those who pay for the vast majority of postal services. Indeed, while the EU level debate stalls, efforts are well underway at national level to corporatize the postal administrations of the Netherlands, the United Kingdom, and Germany. These efforts are generating new pressures to reform European postal policy.

In public speeches these days, prominent officials from the major European postal administrations freely forecast that the postal monopoly will be gone in a decade. Such predictions imply vast changes from current policy, even from those reforms envisioned by the *Green Paper*. On other hand, the formal legal instruments now under consideration retreat from the reform proposals of the last few years. It seems safe to guess that European postal policy will find a compromise between these two polar positions, but hazardous to predict what that compromise will be.

References

Citations to the *Green Paper* and the *Guidelines* are to the section (to assist cross reference to non-English editions) and to the page number of the English edition. Citations to comments included in *Liste* are to the author of the comment cited and to the page number of the original comment as reprinted in *Liste*; the pages of *Liste* is not numbered consecutively. Comments reprinted in *Liste* are in the original language; quotations in the text are presented in unofficial English translation, except for the comments of the Dutch Post Office which were translated by the Dutch Post Office.

Coase, R.H. 1939. "Rowland Hill and the Penny Post," *Economica*: 423, 435.

Codding, George A., Jr. 1964. *The Universal Postal Union.* New York: New York University Press.

Hill, Rowland. 1837. "Post Office Reform."

Crew, Michael A. & Kleindorfer, Paul R., eds. 1991. *Competition and Innovation in Postal Services.* Norwell, Mass.: Kluwer Academic Publishers.

Crew, Michael A. & Kleindorfer, Paul R., eds. 1993. *Regulation and the Nature of Postal and Delivery Services.* Norwell, Mass.: Kluwer Academic Publishers.

European Commission. 1992. *Green Paper on the Development of the Single Market for Postal Services. COM(91) 476 final. Brussels.*

European Commission. 1993. Guidelines for the Development of Community Postal Services, COM(93) 247 final. Brussels.

European Commission. 1993. Liste des Contributions Ecrites Transmises à la Commission Lors de La Periode de Consultation sur le Livre Vert Postal. 2 volumes. Brussels.

European Express Organization. 1990. *Community Delivery Services.* Brussels.

Scheele, Carl H. 1970. *A Short History of the Mail Service.* Washington: Smithsonian Institution Press.

2

DEREGULATION OF AUSTRALIA'S POSTAL SERVICES[1]

Maurice C. Castro

1. Introduction

In November 1993, the Australian Government announced a series of reforms to Australia's postal services and markets. These reforms are the latest in a series which began nearly two decades ago. Until recently, reform had centered on the postal enterprise and on its relationship with its sole owner, the Australian Government. The latest measures however make the first significant changes for a considerable time to the letter monopoly—in other words the services reserved to Australia Post.

At the outset, it should be made clear that the deregulation discussed in this paper involves only a reduction in the regulatory protection afforded the reserved services: deregulation is only partial. However, other decisions of the Government (Beddall 1993a) suggest that further changes in the monopoly can be expected.

This paper describes the evolution of postal reform in Australia over the last two decades, identifies its links with other economy-wide economic policies, considers the future of postal reform in Australia, and concludes with some observations on reform and postal performance.

2. The Postal Enterprise and Its Relationship with the Government

The National Postal Service operated by the Postmaster-General's Department (PMG) came into existence in 1901, following Federation, when the Australian colonies' individual postal administrations were merged. The PMG operated until 1975.

---

1 The views expressed in this paper are those of the author and do not necessarily reflect those of Australia Post or its management.

2.1. The Australian Postal Commission

In 1975, following the Commission of Inquiry into the Australian Post Office (headed by Sir James Vernon), two separate statutory authorities were established, one for telecommunications and one for post. That inquiry followed several years of very poor performance by the postal service. The Australian Postal Commission (the Commission) trading as Australia Post was brought into existence by the Postal Services Act in 1975.

The Commission's main function was to operate postal services with a major social mission. The social objectives were expressed in the legislation as follows:

> ...to best meet the social,industrial and commercial needs of the Australian people for postal services...and make its postal services available throughout Australia for all people who reasonably require those services...[2]

The Commission did not have a commercial charter, although it was required to recover costs and to fund at least half of its capital expenditure requirements. It was also subject to many bureaucratic controls over its day-to-day operations.[3]

2.2. The Australian Postal Corporation

In 1989, the Australian Postal Corporation, still trading as Australia Post, replaced the Australian Postal Commission. The reforms of 1989 included a number of radical changes (Evans 1988). Among these were:

2.2.1. Board of Directors

Persons with the required commercial skill and experience were appointed to the Board and made accountable for performance. Section 79 of the Australian Postal Corporation Act provides for termination of appointments in specified circumstances, including when the performance of the Board or of a particular Director has been unsatisfactory for a significant period of time.

2.2.2. Executive Appointments and Tenure

Starting with top management, executives with private sector commercial experience were recruited and placed on contract. Tenure was abolished, and central government restrictions on payment of market rates were removed.

2.2.3. Clarification of Corporate Objectives

Social objectives were defined and separated from the commercial objectives. Australia Post was required in legislation to operate in accordance with sound commercial practice, including achievement of a reasonable rate of return on assets, payment of all taxes and dividends to the government, and periodic revaluations of assets. It was also required to meet legislated "Community Service Obligations"

---

2 Postal Services Act 1975 (Cwealth), s.7.

3 Postal Services Act, *op cit* ss.74, 76, and 83.

(CSOs) and comply with specified general government policies notified to it from time to time.

2.2.4. Corporate Planning Process

Through the corporate planning process, the Board of Australia Post and the Minister agree on a set of financial, service, and CSO targets over the planning period. The corporate plan which has a three-year time horizon provides the basis for accountability of the Board and top management.

2.2.5. Government Controls

Day-to-day controls such as approval of contracts above a specified value, approval of land purchases, or mandatory Parliamentary review of major postal building works were removed. The government also relaxed certain strategic controls, including central coordination of industrial relations matters.

The 1989 reforms reserved for the government strategic controls over Australia Post, but the day-to-day bureaucratic controls exercised by the Government in earlier periods were abandoned. Through this process of "corporatization," the postal enterprise was placed on a positive commercial footing; and social objectives were now explicitly inserted in the postal enterprise's charter, but their scope, content, and cost impact were specified and quantified. The new framework thus allowed the social and the commercial objectives to be reconciled in an explicitly planned manner.

3. The Regulatory Framework

Australia Post is responsible for the operation of the national postal service. It is wholly owned by the Australian (Federal) Government. The interface between Australia Post and the government is principally through two Ministers: the Minister for Communications and the Arts and the Minister for Finance. The former has responsibility for ongoing postal matters, while the Minister for Finance's role involves oversight of the Government's investments and assets.

Primary responsibility for the commercial operation of the enterprise, including achievement of profits and the payment of dividends to the owner, is the responsibility of the Board of Australia Post. As indicated above, the corporate plan is the vehicle for communicating and agreeing with the Government[4] strategies and policies, including those relating to the Community Service Obligations (CSOs), financial, quality of service and other performance targets, and the cost of the CSOs.

Pricing is the responsibility of Australia Post but is concurrent with a power of "disapproval" available to the Minister *only for the basic postage rate* (the Minister is otherwise unable to issue directions to Australia Post in matters of pricing).[5] Also,

4 Australian Postal Corporation Act 1989 (Cwealth), Division 2.

5 Postal Corporation Act *op cit.* ss.33 and 49.

the prices of all services reserved to Australia Post are subject to the Prices Surveillance Act.[6]

Under the Prices Surveillance Act, Australia Post is required to notify proposed price increases for all the reserved services. The Prices Surveillance Authority administers the Prices Surveillance Act. While it has an advisory role only, it is very influential as it holds public inquiries, and its recommendations are widely publicized.

The basic postage rate which relates to the largest volume domestic letter service, is to be subject to a price capping regime of the form CPI - X from 1994-95.

In relation to competitive conduct and trade practices (fair trading), Australia Post is subject to the Trade Practices Act in respect of its non letter monopoly activities, but not in respect of the letter monopoly.

4. The Letter Monopoly to 1993

Until 1982, the letter monopoly in Australia had followed somewhat similar lines to the arrangements introduced by Rowland Hill in Britain in 1837 (Committee of Inquiry 1982, 38). The letter monopoly reserved for Australia Post all letters up to 500 gms in weight except for letters concerned with goods, and carried with those goods (Committee of Inquiry 1982, 40), and some other minor exceptions.

In 1983, following the report of the Committee of Inquiry Into the Monopoly Position of the Australian Postal Commission (the Bradley Committee), the letter monopoly was relaxed to allow *urgent letters* to be carried by other carriers. The legislation exempted from the monopoly letters carried for a fee at least 10 times the ordinary rate for domestic and overseas letters. Letters up to 500 gms in weight generally continued to be protected by the monopoly.[7]

The Bradley Committee had concluded that a $2 threshold should be legislated to exempt urgent letters from the monopoly. At the time, the basic postage rate was 27 cents. On the important issue of whether or not a natural monopoly existed, interestingly the Bradley Committee stated, it did not consider that "...the theoretical contentions that the postal system constitutes a natural monopoly are persuasive" (Committee of Inquiry 1982, 41).

In support of continuation of the letter monopoly, the Bradley Committee stated:

> ...the Postal Commission's network facilities should not be reduced to an extent which would seriously inconvenience the public and ...the scope and frequency of postal services should be maintained. In particular, the Committee considered that the objectives of the basic letter service in relation to people dwelling or carrying on business outside the cities should not be put at risk (Committee of Inquiry 1982, 44).

---

6 *Ibid* s 32(5) and Prices Surveillance Act 1983 (Cwealth),Declaration under that Act No.75, 5 February 1992.

7 Postal Services Act op cit. s.85.

The letter monopoly was reviewed again in 1992. That review was carried out by the Industry Commission which recommended that it be abolished within five years, if immediate abolition was not acceptable (Industry Commission 1992, xviii). In the event, the Government rejected that advice, but decided to make several changes to the regulatory framework following that inquiry. The main changes are discussed in the following section.

5. The 1994 Postal Reforms

The 1994 postal reforms were announced by the Government in late 1993 (Beddall 1993a) and were based on the Industry Commission report. The reforms are being incorporated in legislation to be introduced in Parliament shortly. Its main elements are as follows:

5.1. Domestic Letter Monopoly

The protected letter monopoly price is to be reduced from 10 times the basic letter rate to 4 times. Based on the current basic postage rate of 45 cents, the threshold is $ 1.80. The weight of protected letters, also, is to be reduced from 500 gms to 250 gms.

Carriage of letters within document exchanges is to be deregulated; and the carriage of mail internal to organizations is to be allowed.

5.2. International Letter Monopoly

Outbound international letter traffic is to be deregulated (but inbound international letters continue to be reserved to Australia Post).

5.3. Downstream Access for Letters (or Interconnection)

A limited access regime for letters (referred to as "interconnection") is to be provided by Australia Post . It involves allowing the carriage by mailers of bulk letters to designated mail centers for *delivery intrastate*, and *the provision of a common discount based on average costs avoided by Australia Post* through the interconnection.

The "interconnection" prices have not yet been submitted to the Prices Surveillance Authority, the pricing regulator for Australia Post's reserved services.

5.4. Further Review of the Letter Monopoly

A review of the remaining limits to competition is to be undertaken in 1996-97.

As a result of these changes, $250 million dollars of Australia Post business will be exposed to competition (Australia Post 1993a). This represents a little under 20 percent of current letter monopoly revenue.

In announcing the Government's decisions, the Minister for Communications stated,

> The Government has agreed to proposals for a sensible managed approach to the introduction of further competition for Australia Post... The initial

> impetus for Australia Post to lift its business performance was given in 1989 when the Government corporatized Australia Post and put in place a commercial charter and board. Australia Post is already the model of a government business enterprise reforming itself. Productivity gains, higher staff morale and strong profits have been the result (Beddall 1993a).

The Minister also stated, in connection with the review in 1996-97:

> The Review should examine the future arrangements for Australia Post. The Review's terms of reference should be consistent with the Government's determinations on the findings of the National Competition Policy Review, including its policies on a declared access regime, monopoly pricing, competitive neutrality and regulatory restrictions on competition (Beddall 1993a).

6. The National Competition Policy Review

The National Competition Policy Review (NCPR) was established with the aim of improving Australia's international competitiveness through a review of institutional impediments to competition at all levels of government (National Competition Policy Review 1993). The Review is best seen as a further development in the government's program of micro economic reform. That program involves the structural adjustment of key industries to achieve sustained longer term growth and improve Australia's competitiveness. NCPR stated "We consider that our proposals are a logical and necessary progression from the national reforms recently implemented in other areas, and that governments (that is both the Federal and State governments in Australia) should give them early attention in the national interest" (National Competition Policy Review 1993). (Statement in brackets added.)

The Council of Australian Governments (which brings together the Federal and State Governments), at a meeting in February 1994 endorsed the recommendations of NCPR subject to some further work being done (Council of Australian Governments 1994). The main recommendations of NCPR followed two major thrusts. The first was to limit the anti-competitive conduct of all firms through extension of the operation of the Trade Practices Act to government owned business enterprises at all levels of government, unincorporated enterprises, and the professions. Most government business enterprises, until now, have been exempt from the Trade Practices Act. The second thrust was aimed at reforming regulation which unjustifiably restricts competition. The reform is to be based on the principles outlined below.

6.1. Public Interest

Any restriction on competition must be demonstrated to be in the public interest. Those making the case for restrictions will be required to support it.

6.2. Process

New proposals for restrictions on competition should be allowed only after close public scrutiny. Restrictions on competition should be limited to five years unless they are extended for a further period of five years following application of the same process.

Existing restrictions on competition should be systematically reviewed for conformity with the public interest principle and be subjected to the same process as described in the preceding paragraph.

6.3. Structural Separation

To facilitate competition, the NCPR proposed reforming public monopolies by changing their structure and achieving three major objectives, as follows:

6.3.1. Regulatory and Commercial Functions

The aim is to separate regulatory and commercial functions. Currently, in many entities, both functions vest in the same bodies.

6.3.2. Natural Monopoly and Competitive Activities

Separate bodies should be established to carry out activities conducted under natural monopoly conditions. Where there are potentially competitive activities carried out in conjunction with natural monopoly activities, the former should be separate and vested in separate entities.

6.3.3. Potentially Competitive Activities

NCPR envisages that potentially competitive activities should be separated into a number of smaller independent business units.

NCPR has expressed a preference for operating units considerably smaller than those currently operating national monopolies. It regards structural separation as an important way of reducing their present market power, and hence, the achievement of a more competitive economy.

6.4. Access to Essential Facilities

NCPR sees a need to ensure third-party access to certain facilities that are essential for competition. A new legal regime is to be established under which firms, in some circumstances, would be given a right of access to specified "essential facilities" on fair and reasonable terms. Key features of the proposed regime include:

6.4.1. Public Inquiries

In the absence of consent by the owner, right of access should be given only after a public inquiry.

6.4.2. Negotiation or Arbitration

The conditions of access would be set at the inquiry for the first term, but subsequently negotiated or arbitrated, if necessary.

6.4.3. National Register

Access agreements would be placed on a national register which would show any additional safeguards to protect the competitive process.

6.5. Price Regulation

NCPR looked to competition to provide pricing discipline in most instances. However, it proposed restraining monopoly pricing behavior through price surveillance. Thus, any firm would become subject to price surveillance, after a public inquiry, and only if it was found to have substantial market power in a substantial market in Australia. The powers would be limited to oversight and monitoring only. The Review recommended against price control.

Price surveillance would be limited to a maximum of three years unless renewed through public inquiry, and all existing price surveillance would lapse within two years unless renewed through public inquiry.

6.6. Competitive Neutrality

NCPR aimed to foster "competitive neutrality" between government and private businesses when they compete. Any advantage which government businesses have had (e.g., exemption from taxation) would be eliminated.

The NCPR further recommended that two new bodies be created to implement its recommendations: the National Competition Council (NCC) and the Australian Competition Commission (ACC). NCC will assist in coordinating cooperative reform (between the States and the federal Governments) and provide independent and expert advice on policy proposals. ACC would be the key administrative body.

7. Performance of Australia Post

Since 1989, Australia Post has shown considerable all round performance. While it is not intended to present here a study of Australia Post's performance over time, four aspects of its performance are used to illustrate the point (Australia Post 1992a; 1992b; 1993b): Tables 1 to 4 in the following pages contain relevant data.

7.1. Price

Table 1 shows movements in the nominal and "real" basic postage 1975-76. A fall of more than one third has occurred since 1975 in the "real" basic postage rate.

7.2. Service Quality

On time delivery is one of the major indicators of letter service quality. Table 2 contains on time delivery measures since 1988. While the measurement of performance was changed in 1992-93 with the introduction of external audit, the results in the table indicate an upward trend in on-time delivery performance over the period.

Table 1. Nominal and Real Basic Postage Rate 1975/76 to 1993/94

Year	Nominal BPR* c	Nominal BPR* Index Sept Qtr, 1975 = 100.0	CPI All Groups 8 Capital Cities* Index Sept Qtr, 1975 = 100.0	Real BPR* Sept Qtr, 1975 = 100	Real BPR* Year on Year Change %
1975/76	18.0	100.0	106.5	0.939	
1976/77	18.0	100.0	121.2	0.825	-12.1%
1977/78	18.0	100.0	132.7	0.754	-8.7%
1978/79	20.0	111.1	143.6	0.774	2.7%
1979/80	21.0	116.7	158.1	0.738	-4.6%
1980/81	22.0	122.2	173.0	0.706	-4.3%
1981/82	24.8	137.8	191.0	0.721	2.1%
1982/83	27.0	150.0	213.0	0.704	-2.4%
1983/84	29.3	162.8	227.5	0.716	1.6%
1984/85	31.5	175.0	237.2	0.738	3.1%
1985/86	33.0	183.3	257.2	0.713	-3.3%
1986/87	36.0	200.0	281.2	0.711	-0.3%
1987/88	37.0	205.6	301.8	0.681	-4.2%
1988/89	38.5	213.9	324.1	0.660	-3.1%
1989/90	41.0	227.8	350.1	0.651	-1.4%
1990/91	43.0	238.9	368.3	0.649	-0.3%
1991/92	44.0	244.4	375.3	0.651	0.4%
1992/93	45.0	250.0	379.1	0.659	1.2%
1993/94	45.0	250.0	386.4	0.647	-1.9%

Sources:

Australian Bureau of Statistics, Consumer Price Index, Cat. No. 6401.0, various

Australia Post, Post Charges, MS11, various

*Average for the year

Table 2. Delivery Performance 1989 to 1993—Within Promised Time

	Percent Delivered on Time
1988/89	89
1989/90	88
1990/91	94
1991/92	96
1992/93*	92.3
1993/94**	93.9

Sources:

Australia Post, and since March quarter 1993 externally audited performance by KPMG Peat Marwick.

*New performance measurement/audit introduced in second half of the year.

**Part year results.

7.3. Productivity

Labor productivity is frequently used as an indicator of efficiency in the delivery of postal services. The process is very labor-intensive and labor productivity captures most of the improvements made.

Table 3 shows annual changes in labor productivity since 1975. Over the period, productivity change has shown consistent, though variable, improvement. Since 1990-91, a significant change in the trend occurred, with the annual rate of change increasing and performance reaching relatively high levels.

Table 3. Labor Productivity Revenue at Constant Prices per Paid Workyear 1975/76 to 1992/93

Year	Revenue at Constant Prices per Paid Workyear Index 1975/76 = 100	Annual Productivity Change %
1975/76	1.000	
1976/77	1.053	5.3%
1977/78	1.059	0.6%
1978/79	1.091	3.0%
1979/80	1.116	2.3%
1980/81	1.137	1.9%
1981/82	1.161	2.1%
1982/83	1.183	1.9%
1983/84	1.191	0.6%
1984/85	1.191	0.0%
1985/86	1.194	0.3%
1986/87	1.237	3.6%
1987/88	1.287	4.0%
1988/89	1.347	4.7%
1989/90	1.339	-0.6%
1990/91	1.375	2.7%
1991/92	1.421	3.3%
1992/93	1.495	5.2%

Source: Australia Post

7.4. Profitability

Table 4 shows Australia Post's profitability since 1975. Profitability trended upwards starting in 1989-90 reflecting the reforms outlined in this paper.

In brief, Australia Post since 1989 has held or reduced the real price of its output, improved service quality, raised its productivity, and increased its profitability. Not illustrated in the charts but a fact, nevertheless, is that it has continued to meet its social obligations as required in its enabling legislation.

Table 4. Corporate Annual Profit 1975/76 to 1992/93

Year	Annual Profit* $M
1975/76	31.6
1976/77	28.9
1977/78	2.0
1978/79	22.6
1979/80	11.7
1980/81	-12.7
1981/82	0.8
1982/83	0.4
1983/84	24.1
1984/85	24.4
1985/86	30.8
1986/87	54.8
1987/88	54.9
1988/89	46.2
1989/90	71.3
1990/91	146.2
1991/92	178.7
1992/93	249.4

Source: Australia Post

* Operating profit before abnormals and income tax

8. Future Postal Reform in Australia

The past twenty years have seen several waves of postal reform in Australia; and it is fair to say that reform has been generally successful. As an enterprise, Australia Post has improved its performance markedly following the changes made to its status, structure, and its relationship with the Government in the dual capacity of sole owner and regulator. Furthermore, from a public policy point of view, the social objectives set by the Government have been consistently met, and the retention of national assets in the postal enterprise has been well justified.

While the drivers of postal reform in the 1970s were industry specific, since the late 1980s, postal reform has been part of a national all-industries strategy. Increasingly, therefore, developments in the postal area are being affected by, as well as influencing, reform in other Australian industries.

Government statements in relation to the NCPR (Beddall 1993a) and the continuing imperative to improve Australia's international competitiveness indicate strong pressure for change will continue to be felt in all service areas.

A major milestone in future postal reform is the Review of future arrangements for Australia Post scheduled to begin in July 1996. As indicated earlier, this review will be undertaken in light of the Government's decisions regarding NCPR. The government's announcement stated:

> The Review's terms of reference should be consistent with the Government's determinations on the findings of the National Competition Policy Review, including its policies on a declared access regime, competitive neutrality and regulatory restrictions on competition.
>
> This is consistent with the Government's view that a public monopoly must justify the continuation of its monopoly position (Beddall 1993a).

It seems likely therefore that the 1996-97 review will examine the implications of the Industry Commission's proposition that reserved services protection is necessary to ensure the uniform charge for standard letters continues and is funded by cross subsidy from low cost to high cost mail paths (Industry Commission 1992, 216).

The extent of monopoly protection may be reconsidered in terms of the weight and price at which competition will be allowed. As well, the scope of the monopoly may be examined in terms of the types of communications to be excluded from the reserved services.

The "natural monopoly" issue may also be revisited, and with it, the form of regulation which might be appropriate. The NCPR report has signalled the need to address issues of structural separation, and that generic rather than specific regulation would be preferred. The overall model favored is one which would generally reserve specialist regulatory agencies for very limited technical purposes, for example the regulation of air safety or the management of radio frequencies. The Australian Competition Commission would be the competition watchdog with administration, oversight, and monitoring powers in relation to all sectors of the economy (National Competition Policy Review 1993, 356-357).

Other aspects of regulation which were raised by the NCPR report are control of monopoly prices through light-handed oversight or monitoring of prices—not price control, presumably with the assistance of price caps of the CPI - X type (National Competition Policy Review 1993, 280) already mandated in the 1993 postal reform package. However, NCPR, as indicated above, has also advocated the creation of access rights to "essential facilities." As already noted, a limited access regime was part of the 1994 postal reforms.

Examination has been scheduled of aspects of Australia Post's Community Service Obligations (CSOs).The Government has announced a review of postal services to residents of rural and remote areas of Australia, to be undertaken by a Parliamentary Committee once in the life of each Parliament, starting early next year (Lee and Woods 1994).

Funding of Australia Post's CSOs has been by internal cross subsidy, but a variety of alternative funding methods for CSOs in other services are currently in use in Australia. For example, direct budget subsidy, or payment from an industry trust fund where more than one producer operates, or on the basis of performance contracts with the government. The Industry Commission had proposed that Australia Post's CSOs be funded by direct budget subsidy based on criteria of transparency, clarity, and incentives for efficient behavior (Industry Commission 1992, 125-126).

In 1992, the Industry Commission had also proposed that Australia Post be privatized at the completion of a five-year reform process (Industry Commission 1992, xxii). The then Minister for Communications, David Beddall, in a speech to the Postal Conference (Beddall 1993b) stated the Government's approach was built around "...encouraging Australia Post to operate at world's best practice...as a 100% publicly owned corporation."

9. Reform and Performance

Performance of a business as complex as that of Australia Post is normally subject to many factors and influences; it is therefore very difficult to attribute causality to any single factor.

Clearly the performance of Australia Post since 1989 has shown considerable improvement. While this improvement has coincided with the introduction of reforms, it still leaves somewhat open the question of the relationship of reform and performance.

This is a difficult question, but some useful inferences may still be drawn.

The reforms were given high visibility when they were announced, and again when they were introduced. This had a marked psychological impact on all those involved: management, the workforce, and postal customers. The philosophical underpinnings of reform could be communicated and promoted, and this helped to set the tone for better performance all round.

On a more tangible level and from an internal perspective, the more important factors behind the lift in performance have been the clear commercial focus and the clarification of objectives with the Government. Associated with these changes, a major culture change involving the workforce in a participative approach to work management down to the "shop floor" was also a major determinant of performance.

From the perspective of market deregulation, it is too early to form a view since the first phase of deregulation has not yet commenced. However, Australia Post is well placed to face such an increase in competition both due to its stronger commercial position following successful internal reform and because this first deregulation step follows "...a sensible, managed approach to the introduction of further competition..." (Beddall 1993a) by the Government.

References

Australian Postal. 1992a. *Submission to the Industry Commission Inquiry Into Mail Courier and Parcel Services*. Australia Post, Melbourne (February).

Australia Post. 1992b. *Annual Report 1991/92.*

Australia Post. 1993a. *Industry Commission Outcome, The Government's Decision and How We'll Meet the Challenge*. Melbourne (December).

Australia Post. 1993b. *Annual Report 1992/93.*

Beddall, D. 1993a. *Sensible Approach Preferred in Postal Reforms.* Minister for Communications, Media Release 40/93 (November 15).

Beddall, D. 1993b. *Postal Policy, A Changing Postal System.* Speech by the Hon. David Beddall MP, Minister for Communications, to the Postal Reform Conference, AIC Conferences, Sydney (December 1).

Committee of Inquiry Into the Monopoly Position of the Australian Postal Commission. 1982. *Report.* Australian Government Publishing Service, Canberra.

Council of Australian Governments. 1994. *Communiqué.* Hobart (February 25).

Evans, G., 1988. *Reshaping the Transport and Communications Government Business Enterprises.* Statement by the Minister for Transport and Communications, Australian Government Publishing Service, Canberra.

Industry Commission. 1992. *Mail Courier and Parcel Services.* Report No. 28, Australian Government Publishing Services, Canberra.

Lee, Michael, and Harry Woods. 1994. *Postal Working Party Report.* Joint Media Release by the Minister for Communications and the Arts and the Convenor, Country Mail Services Working Party, Harry Woods, MP, Canberra.

National Competition Policy Review. 1993. *Report of the Independent Committee of Inquiry.* Australian Government Publishing Service, Canberra (August).

COMMENTS

John Haldi

1. Introduction

From the perspective of postal economics, Australia is interesting because it is amongst those countries in the vanguard of postal deregulation. This paper does an excellent job of reporting on and summarizing recent postal developments in Australia. It is lucid and succinct, two highly commendable qualities.

One really cannot fault the facts and description presented in this paper. The author might, however, have given more attention to certain topics that strike me as worth further exploration, and this is where these comments are directed.

2. The 1989 Corporate Reform

The major reform enacted to date was government's decision to convert the previous Australian Postal Commission to the Australian Postal Corporation in 1989. This was not privatization. Nor did the door to direct competition in delivery services crack open even a little. At that stage of reform, the monopoly on services historically reserved to Australia Post remained firmly intact.

Monopoly gives an organization the luxury of not having to be economically efficient—the luxury of a quiet life, so to speak. Did Australia Post fail to operate along the efficiency frontier prior to 1989? The data and other information presented are not sufficient to reach such a conclusion. In light of the significant and continuing improvements reported to have occurred since 1989, however, it seems clear that if Australia Post was operating at or near the efficiency frontier prior to that time, remarkable strides have been made at pushing the frontier back.

Since the postal monopoly remained firmly intact after 1989, the steady improvement exhibited by the Postal Corporation may appear somewhat surprising. As the author notes, improvement has *coincided* with introduction of reforms, which "therefore raises the question of the relationship of the reforms to performance." He is a bit succinct when he says "executives with private sector commercial experience were recruited" and "tenure was abolished." Was the previous hand of government so heavy that merely lifting this weight from the organization enabled great advances to occur? Although we may well suspect the answer, the author could usefully have summarized the more important sources of productivity and service gains and analyzed them in relation to the corporate reform. For example,

- What government controls were most oppressive?
- Were old-line managers, totally accustomed to a "government-style" operation, the key problem?
- Was Australia Post prevented from investing in new equipment with high payoffs because of government budgetary constraints or controls on capital expenditures?
- When government "corporatized" Australia Post, how did the internal incentive and reward structure change?
- Did the Corporation close large numbers of costly retail outlets, or convert previously owned post offices to contract stations?
- Was frequency of deliveries to rural areas curtailed?[1]
- Did elimination of tenure and political constraints enable a reduction in staffing levels or wage rates?
- Could other governments emulate or adopt the essential advances and improvements made by Australia Post without converting to a corporate form of organization?

More discussion on the key lessons to be learned from Australia's experience in adopting a corporate form of organization would be of considerable value for many other countries when they get around to reviewing their own postal administration.

3. The 1994 Reforms and Australia Post's View of Competition

Another topic, perhaps a bit sensitive for the author to discuss, is the controversy surrounding government's decision to reduce the scope of services reserved to Australia Post. In a vigorous defense of its monopoly, Australia Post (1992a, 1992b) rounded up all the usual suspects.

The featured centerpiece was the universal service obligation at a uniform price, as might be expected. Also featured, should government eliminate or severely curtail the postal monopoly, was the customary vision of looming disaster. Cream-skimming[2] would assuredly arise and, in general, the sky could certainly be expected to fall. Meaning, of course, Australia Post's revenues, profits, and employment would fall, and the company would be unable to meet its Community Service Obligations to serve rural customers.

Nowhere does the author discuss the fact that in the United States private couriers have adopted uniform pricing for delivery anywhere within the 48 contiguous states. Courier companies do compete on service and price (e.g., negotiated quantity discounts), but rates quoted are uniform for delivery everywhere in the 48 states, including rural areas somewhat distant from airports utilized by the couriers.

1 In Australia, some rural areas receive delivery only one or two days a week.

2 For obvious reasons, Australia Post did not point out that entry of cream-skimmers means that a number of its customers will no longer be "creamed."

Australia is a big country, but the United States also encompasses long distances and sparsely populated areas. Sooner or later, monopolists' ceaseless cry of "cream skimming" must be confronted with these realities of the marketplace. Courier companies do not make money on every single delivery. Every day, deliveries to some addressees are probably "cross-subsidized." Yet private courier companies make no attempt to revise their pricing structure to earn a profit on each and every delivery. Instead, the cross-subsidized deliveries can be likened to "loss leaders" which couriers use to attract other, highly profitable business.

Australia Post also trumpets the old refrain of "no one else is doing it." Perhaps they had not heard of Finland, Holland, New Zealand, or Sweden. These postal administrations have wholeheartedly embraced relaxation and even elimination of the statutory monopoly on letter mail. Moreover, they all appear to be succeeding quite well with few or no reserved services, thus showing that the entire panoply of postal services may indeed be contestable.

Although the author ably describes the pending reforms, he regrettably does not prognosticate on their likely effects. Specifically, after the scope of reserved services is reduced, will mailers be better served? And will performance of Australia Post improve further, or will erosion of the monopoly and vigorous competition by private sector competitors push Australia Post into the vicious spiral of eroding service and increasing prices? Unfortunately, there are few clues or hints as to whether the specter of increased competition is likely to drive future improvements in performance.

One important reform will be the establishment of downstream access for letters. On the basis of experience in the United States, I would hazard the following prediction. After Australia Post establishes discounts for intrastate delivery, it will also open the door to various other worksharing activities by mailers, such as presortation, prebarcoding, etc. Australia Post will then discover that for each $1.00 in avoided costs it will need to forgo only 70 to 90 cents in revenues. The somewhat ironic conclusion is that this forced relaxation of the reserved service will end up making Australia Post financially stronger, not weaker.

4. Some Paradoxical Results Concerning the Alleged Burden of Universal Service at a Uniform Price

Cohen, Ferguson and Xenakis (1993) in their study of rural delivery in the United States, claim that a *comprehensive* delivery network, including the rural portion, has *great value*. They point to alternate delivery carriers and telephone companies as analogous situations where firms strive to provide all-inclusive service. Dominant firms use comprehensive networks as an effective selling and marketing tool to promote one-stop shopping.

On the basis of my own research, Cohen, Ferguson, and Xenakis are absolutely correct insofar as the United States is concerned. Owing to high per capita mail volumes in the United States, virtually every rural route has the potential to recover all direct costs and even contribute meaningfully to overhead costs. No rational profit maximizing firm would abandon such routes.

In stark contrast, Australia Post believes its Community Service Obligations impose a great cost and burden, and forcing it to maintain a comprehensive delivery network *reduces value*. These conflicting viewpoints need to be reconciled.

Both views may possibly be correct, each in their own context. In Australia the population is more sparse than in the United States, and mail volume per household is lower. When population is too sparse, or mail volume per household is too low, provision of rural delivery service may fail to recover direct costs and, hence, require a cross-subsidy. But the United States experience demonstrates that rural routes need not require a cross-subsidy. One businesslike approach to this situation is for postal administrations to promote their business aggressively and seek growth in mail volume. The widely disparate mail volume per capita between countries indicates considerable untapped potential is probably available for exploitation.

The issue of whether universal service is economic extends far beyond Australia. European countries far more densely populated than Australia are linked by modern transportation networks and highway systems. In the context of these countries, the intellectual challenges that need to be addressed are: (1) How much density and what volume of mail are required to make rural routes self-sufficient (i.e., recover direct costs)? and (2) Must rural routes be completely self-sufficient before they add value to a network organization? If universal service is in fact economic, then the universal service obligation is no reason to preserve reserved services.

5. Concluding Remarks

Postal administrations in Finland, Holland, New Zealand, and Sweden have taken the lead in allowing market demands to shape the services supplied by postal providers. In comparison with these countries, Australia is not a leader in deregulation. Still, it is in the vanguard of countries where government is forcing the postal administration to accept more competition and adapt to market dictates. At this time, Australia seems comfortably ahead of the latest round of reforms being circulated within the European Common Market. Hopefully, Australia Post will succeed admirably, lose its fear of competition, and become an enthusiastic supporter of competitive postal markets.

References

Australia Postal Corporation. 1992a. *Submission to the Industry Commission Inquiry into Mail, Courier and Parcel Services*. February.

Australia Postal Corporation. 1992b. *Response to the Industry Commission Draft Report on the inquiry into Mail, Courier and Parcel Services*. September.

Cohen, Robert H., William F. Ferguson, and Spyros S. Xenakis. 1993. "Rural Delivery and the Universal Service Obligation: A Quantitative Investigation." In *Regulation and the Nature of Postal and Delivery Services,* edited by Michael A. Crew and Paul Kleindorfer. Boston: Kluwer Academic Publishers.

3

THE APPLICATION OF LEGAL SAFEGUARDS AGAINST PREDATION TO THE POSTAL SERVICES INDUSTRY[1]

William E. Kovacic

Introduction

The emergence of an increasingly competitive market for postal and delivery services is raising a variety of competition policy issues concerning the relationship between traditional, regulated incumbent service providers and new entrants (Campbell 1993; Sherman 1991). The recent history of other regulated industries that have experienced increased competition indicates that government policymakers will confront difficult issues concerning how dominant incumbent postal service providers may respond to entry (Kahn 1992). Dominant incumbents can be expected to react by cutting prices for competitive services, seeking to restrict access to "bottleneck" facilities, devising new products, and engaging in aggressive promotional campaigns.

Experience with the transition from regulation to competition in other public utility sectors tells us that incumbent responses to new entry (or expansion by fringe firms) will lead rival service providers to attack the incumbents' defensive strategies as unlawfully exclusionary. Standards developed through the interpretation of the antitrust laws of the affected countries will provide one set of analytical tools for evaluating claims of unlawful exclusion. This paper considers how competition policy concepts developed under the antitrust laws of the European Community (EC) and the United States might be applied to resolve claims of predation that arise in the postal services sector. It focuses upon standards designed to control dominant firm pricing behavior and refusals to deal with competitors.

The paper addresses the topic in three parts. The first part describes exclusionary

1 The author is grateful to James Campbell, Brona Carlton, Michael Crew, Kathryn Fenton, Per Forssberg, Wynne Jones, Paul Kleindorfer, John Panzar, Frank Pieper, Paul Richards, David Sibbick, David Storer, Ulrich Stumpf, and Sture Wallander for many useful comments and discussions. The author also thanks the John M. Olin Foundation and the Sarah Scaife Foundation for their generous financial support.

conduct issues that will arise in the EC and the United States as rivalry among postal service providers increases. The second section outlines the regulatory framework through which competition policy principles developed under antitrust statutes can be applied to allegations of unlawful exclusion in the EC and the United States. The third section discusses existing EC and United States antitrust principles that may be applied by courts and postal services regulators to evaluate the response of incumbent postal firms to new entry.

1. The Postal Services Industry and Exclusionary Conduct Issues

Competition is an increasingly prominent feature of the postal services market. Among other forces, the emergence of private courier services and the growing use of facsimile transmission have placed enormous pressure upon the operations and revenues of national postal firms (Crew and Kleindorfer 1992, 11, 119). There is every reason to expect that competitive inroads into what once was the exclusive domain of national postal firms will increase in the foreseeable future (Dobbenberg 1992).

Modern experience with other public utility sectors that have moved from a condition of regulated monopoly to a more competitive environment gives a reliable basis for identifying competition policy issues that will arise as rivalry intensifies in the postal sector. One major illustration is the transformation of the telecommunications industry, whose structural characteristics bear important similarities to the postal services industry (Crew and Kleindorfer 1992, 1-3; Panzar 1992). AT&T's efforts in the 1960s and 1970s to repel entrants in markets for long-distance service and telecommunications equipment raised difficult competition policy issues for public utility regulators (such as the Federal Communications Commission) and confronted courts with many antitrust challenges to AT&T's pricing and equipment interconnection policies. An antitrust suit by the U.S. Department of Justice ultimately led to the divestiture of AT&T's local service and equipment manufacturing operations from its long distance operations.[2] And

2 See United States v. AT&T Co., 552 F. Supp. 131 (D.D.C. 1982) (entering antitrust consent decree requiring the restructuring of the Bell System), aff'd sub nom. Maryland v. United States, 460 U.S. 1001 (1983); Temin (1987, 108-90) (discussing Justice Department's antitrust suit against AT&T); see also Southern Pacific Communications Co. v. AT&T Co., 740 F.2d 980 (D.C. Cir. 1984) (antitrust challenge to AT&T's pricing conduct), cert. denied, 470 U.S. 1005 (1985); MCI Communications Corp. v. AT&T Co., 708 F.2d 1081 (7th Cir.) (antitrust challenge to AT&T's pricing and service interconnection policies), cert. denied, 464 U.S. 891 (1983); Northeastern Tel. Co. v. AT&T Co., 651 F.2d 76 (2d Cir. 1981) (antitrust challenge to AT&T's pricing and equipment interconnection policies), cert. denied, 455 U.S. 943 (1982); cf. British Telecommunications, O. J. L 360/36 (Dec. 21, 1982), CCH ¶ 10,443, aff'd sub nom. Italian Republic v. Commission, 1985 E.C.R. 510, *Common Market Reporter* (CCH) ¶ 14,168 (finding an abuse of a dominant market position under Article 86 of the Treaty of Rome where British Telecommunications barred private-message forwarding agencies from relaying telex messages received from and intended for other countries).

competition in the post-divestiture telecommunications market has sown the seeds of future disputes concerning the demands of new service providers for access to the local distribution networks owned by the Regional Bell Operating Companies (Baumol and Sidak 1994; Larson et al. 1994).

Three principal competition problems will command attention in the postal services sector. The first deals with incumbent firm decisions concerning pricing and the introduction of new products. As rival service providers (such as specialized courier companies) take sales away from the incumbent national postal carrier, the incumbent is likely to drop prices on competing services or offer new products that mimic those of its competitors. As the incumbent postal company cuts prices or introduces new products, the entrant often will fear that the low price or new product does not cover its costs and is being subsidized by revenues from products for which the incumbent still holds a monopoly franchise. These fears are likely to result in claims of predatory pricing by means of cross-subsidization.[3] Claims of illegal below-cost pricing also could arise in disputes between rival private couriers as such entities compete for an increased share of international delivery transactions.[4]

The second problem involves access to what antitrust specialists call "bottleneck" or "essential" facilities (Baker 1993; Kovacic 1992a). Most students of postal economics regard the local delivery network as having natural monopoly characteristics (Owen and Willig 1983; Panzar 1991; Rogerson and Takis 1992). As the gatekeeper to this natural monopoly network, incumbent dominant firms have considerable ability to determine the competitive fortunes of rivals by setting the terms for access to the network. Where the monopolist either refuses to provide access to the local delivery network, or grants access only on terms that its rivals regard as excessively onerous, rival service providers are likely to claim that access restrictions constitute unlawfully exclusionary behavior.[5]

---

3 See Air Courier Conference v. United States Postal Service, 959 F.2d 1213 (3d Cir. 1992) (describing claims of predatory pricing raised by an association of private courier services against the U.S. Postal Service in connection with the decision by USPS to cut the price for its international Express Mail service); see also EC Green Paper (1992, 174) ("A particularly important aspect is the use by postal administrations of the same network to provide both reserved services and non-reserved services. Evidently, there could be a danger here of unfair cross-subsidies from the reserved sector which would enable the postal administrations to offer non-reserved services at prices below their proper cost."); cf. Sievers and Albery (1992) (discussing possibilities for multiproduct regulated firms to prey upon new entrants by manipulating the allocation of overhead costs).

4 The establishment of a borderless, single EC market has increased the demand for private courier services and intensified competition among United States and European courier firms. See Patrick Oster, "In Europe, U.S. Shippers Shoot Ahead," *Washington Post*, June 11, 1993, at D1.

5 See also Dobbs and Richards (1992) (discussing pricing issues associated with allowing entrants access to existing postal networks); EC Green Paper (1992, 174-75) (addressing importance of access criteria); Stumpf (1992) (discussing conditions of access by remailers to inward delivery networks of national postal administrations).

The third area of concern involves the distinction between "reserved" postal services, for which the national postal administration holds a legal monopoly and has the right to exclude all other entities from providing such services, and "unreserved" services, which private firms lawfully can offer in competition with the national postal administration. National postal companies (or interest groups such as postal unions that benefit from the suppression of competition) may seek the adoption of a broad definition of reserved services and may initiate legal proceedings to restrict private firms that seek to offer services in areas that arguably fall within the field of reserved activities.[6] In several instances since the early 1980s, the Commission of the European Community has used the competition articles of the Treaty of Rome to investigate efforts by several EC member states to define express services as reserved activities and therefore falling within the national postal authority's legal monopoly (EC Green Paper 1992, 56-57; Krause 1986, 54-61).[7]

2. Legal Framework Governing Exclusionary Conduct by Incumbents

An elaborate array of national and international legal controls governs the ability of incumbent postal firms to exclude or restrict competition from rival service providers. The basic ingredients of this legal scheme are sketched below.[8]

---

6 See, e.g., Procureur du Roi v. Corbeau, Case C-320/91 (Court of Justice: May 19, 1993) (not yet published) (ruling that Article 90 of the Treaty of Rome bars enforcement of a postal monopoly statute to sanction a private service provider where the postal authority does not provide the services in question, where the services are separable from services operated by the postal authority in the general interest, and where the provision of private services does not jeopardize the economic stability of postal authority services operated in the general interest).

7 See also *Corbeau*, Case C-320/91 (interpreting limits imposed by Article 90 of Treaty of Rome upon enforcement of postal monopoly statute against provider of special collection and delivery services); compare Air Courier Conference v. American Postal Workers Union, 111 S. Ct. 913 (1991) (concluding that American Postal Workers Union lacked standing to challenge decision by U.S. Postal Service to issue a rule that suspended the operation of the Private Express Statutes and permitted private courier services to engage in certain international remailing activities); American Postal Services Union v. React Postal Services, Inc., 771 F.2d 1375 (10th Cir. 1985) (rejecting argument by American Postal Workers Union that Private Express Statutes forbade a private company from presorting and carrying its customers' letters from its letter collection boxes, aggregating the letters according to business addressees, and mailing the aggregated letters through the U.S. Postal Service); U.S. Postal Service v. O'Brien, 644 F. Supp. 140 (D.D.C. 1986) (relying on Private Express Statutes to enjoin private courier service from delivery of "non-urgent" letters where the courier service delivered both urgent and non-urgent letters).

8 For a more comprehensive treatment of the legal framework governing postal services competition within EC member states, see EC Green Paper (1992, 37-61).

2.1. National Controls

Each nation's postal monopoly is defined by a collection of legal commands that set the bounds of reserved services dedicated to the national postal authority. The content of these legal governance structures varies from country to country. For example, the dimensions of the postal monopoly in Germany are fixed by the interaction of constitutional provisions and statutes that create the Deutsche Bundespost and enumerate its powers (Stumpf 1991). As Section 2.2 explains below, the reach of competition-suppressing constitutional provisions and statutes is limited by international agreements, including the competition provisions of the Treaty of Rome.

A different legal framework delineates the monopoly held by the United States Postal Service (USPS). The USPS monopoly is established in the Postal Reorganization Act of 1970.[9] The 1970 Reorganization Act codified the United States postal monopoly in a group of statutes known as the Private Express Statutes, which generally prohibit private companies from offering collection and delivery services that compete against USPS.[10] Violations of the Private Express Statutes are punishable through criminal fines or imprisonment.[11] The Private Express Statutes authorize USPS to suspend restrictions against private carriage "upon any mail route where the public interest requires the suspension."[12] In several instances USPS has used this power to allow competitive entry by private service providers. For example, in 1979 USPS adopted a rule permitting private courier services to offer overnight delivery for "extremely urgent letters."[13]

The 1970 Reorganization Act also limits the discretion of USPS to set prices in response to competition from private service providers. The Act states that "[p]ostal rates shall be established to apportion the costs of all postal operations to all users of the mail on a fair and equitable basis."[14] The Act further requires USPS to "plan, develop, promote, and provide adequate and efficient postal services at fair and reasonable rates and fees,"[15] and bars USPS from setting rates that "make any undue or unreasonable discrimination among users of the mails."[16] American courts generally have concluded that private competitors of USPS have standing to sue USPS for failures to satisfy these standards. Thus, a private courier service could invoke the 1970 Reorganization requirement that USPS charge "fair and reasonable" rates to challenge USPS for charging an unreasonably low price for a service for which USPS faces private competition.

---

9 Public Law 91-375, 84 Stat. 727 (1970). On the history of the postal monopoly in the United States, see Craig and Alvis (1977); Priest (1975).

10 39 U.S.C. §§ 601-606.

11 18 U.S.C. §§ 1693-1699.

12 39 U.S.C. § 601(b).

13 See 44 Fed. Reg. 61178 (1979), codified at 39 C.F.R. § 320.6 (1993).

14 39 U.S.C. § 101(d).

15 39 U.S.C. § 403(a).

16 39 U.S.C. § 403(c).

The United States antitrust laws (notably, Section 2 of the Sherman Act, which bars attempted monopolization and monopolization[17]) do not constrain USPS in responding to competitive entry. The American antitrust statutes do not apply to the conduct of federal government entities (American Bar Association 1992, 964-65), a classification that includes USPS. However, such statutes would apply to the conduct of private firms, such as private courier services that engage in aggressive pricing policies to subdue other private courier services. In addition, a future decision to privatize USPS likely would render USPS subject to the U.S. antitrust laws.

2.2. International Controls

A number of international agreements and rulemaking processes regulate the market for postal services. These include the Universal Postal Union, the General Agreement on Tariffs and Trade, and the Conference of European Postal and Telecommunications Administrations (Campbell 1992; EC Green Paper 1992, 51-53). For competition policy purposes, the most important international constraint upon the conduct of postal service entities (especially in EC member states) is the Treaty of Rome and its competition provisions (Articles 85 to 94). As a general principle, national postal authorities responsible for providing reserved services must abide by Treaty of Rome competition mandates such as Article 85, which prohibits cartel-like conduct, and Article 86, which forbids the abuse of a dominant market position. Article 90 of the Treaty addresses the duties of public undertakings, such as national postal administrations, under Articles 85 and 86. Article 90(1) bars EC member states from enacting or enforcing measures that contradict the Treaty's requirements. This provision does not ban government monopolies, but Article 90(2) tolerates such entities only where their operation does not impede the development of trade (EC Green Paper 1992, 55; Krause 1986, 51).

The Commission of the European Community has used Article 90 to initiate investigations or cases involving a number of competition policy issues dealing with the relationship between national postal authorities and private entrants. Subject matter of Commission inquiries has included the proper delineation of reserved postal services, direct prohibitions upon remailing, and the setting of terminal dues in a manner that served to inhibit remailing activities by private firms (Green Paper 1992, 55-57; Krause 1986, 54-61). In addition, the Commission in 1985 applied the Treaty of Rome's competition articles to obtain assurances from the Deutsche Bundespost that it would not respond to new competition from private couriers in the express mail market by charging prices below its costs for express delivery services.[18]

The Court of Justice of the European Communities recently invoked Article 90 to identify limits on the use of national postal monopoly laws to block private entry.

17 15 U.S.C. § 2.

18 Commission P.R., IP (85) 10 (Jan. 18, 1985).

In *Procureur du Roi v. Corbeau*,[19] the Court responded to a request by the Belgian Tribunal Correctionnel for a preliminary ruling in connection with a criminal case against Paul Corbeau, who was alleged to have infringed the Belgian Post Office's legal monopoly by providing special mail collection and distribution services. The Court recognized that the obligation of the holder of a state-granted exclusive franchise to provide its services presupposed the cross-subsidization of less profitable activities by more profitable activities. This obligation justified limits on entry into profitable lines of business, consistent with Article 90. However, the Court held that Article 90 precluded legislative protection against competition where (1) the monopolist incumbent did not supply the services in question, (2) the challenged services were separable from services provided by the monopolist incumbent in the general interest, and (3) private provision of the disputed services would not jeopardize the economic stability of services operated in the general interest by the monopolist. The High Court left for the referring court (the Tribunal Correctionnel) the task of determining whether Corbeau's services satisfied these conditions.

3. Competition Standards Governing Predation

The application of United States and EC antitrust statutes has generated a large body of case law and academic literature concerning the appropriate standards for evaluating claims of unlawful exclusion against dominant firms. The results of modern judicial and academic efforts to devise exclusionary conduct rules are likely to guide courts and regulators as they examine claims of predation in the postal services market. The discussion below identifies elements of exclusionary conduct jurisprudence and scholarly analysis that have important implications for postal service providers.

3.1. Exclusionary Conduct Defined

In conceptual terms, courts and commentators largely agree about the characteristics that distinguish harmful dominant firm exclusionary behavior from desirable competitive conduct. Robert Bork (1978, 144) defines predation as a "firm's deliberate aggression against one or more rivals through the employment of business practices that would not be considered profit maximizing" except for one of two expectations: (a) that the conduct will drive competitors from the market, which would give the predator the ability to raise prices and command monopoly profits, or (b) through fear or a renewed spirit of cooperation, competitors will "abandon competitive behavior that the predator finds inconvenient or threatening."

Although his policy preferences differ greatly from Bork's, Lawrence Sullivan (1977, 111) defines predation in similar terms:

19 Case C-320/91 (Court of Justice: May 19, 1993) (not yet published).

> [T]he predator seeks not to win the field by greater efficiency, better services, or lower prices reflective of cost savings or modest profits. The predatory firm tries to inhibit others in ways independent of the predator's own ability to perform effectively in the market. Its price reduction or predatory expenditure is calculated to impose losses on other firms, not to garner gains for itself; indeed, the predation is likely to involve present losses to the predator, or at all events to foreclose profits which could currently be earned, detriments which are accepted by the predator as the cost of freeing itself for the future from the competition it now faces.

The cause of disagreement among courts and academics is not the general definition of predation, but the appropriate content of the operational criteria for addressing the general phenomenon. The issue of operational tests is treated below with respect to dominant firm pricing behavior and requests for access to essential facilities under the dominant firm's control.

3.2. Dominant Firm Pricing Controls

The past twenty years have produced extraordinary ferment in judicial and scholarly analysis of predatory pricing allegations (Hurwitz and Kovacic 1983; Larson and Kovacic 1990). To an extent unequalled in other areas of competition law, the research of industrial organization economists and antitrust attorneys has led courts to reshape legal standards governing claims of exclusionary pricing.

3.2.1. Academic Schools of Thought

Commentators have proposed essentially four approaches to dealing with allegations of predatory pricing by dominant firms (Larson and Kovacic 1990, 4-8; OECD 1988). The first is the cost-based school, which argues that the relationship of the dominant firm's prices to its costs should be the primary tool for identifying unlawful pricing. The most influential cost-based rule has been devised by Philip Areeda and Donald Turner (1975; 1978, ¶ 711), who propose that pricing by a monopolist below its average variable cost be treated as unlawful and that pricing at or above average variable cost be deemed legal.

The second approach is the structural filter school. This school accepts the potential usefulness of cost-based tests, but argues that such standards should be applied only after the court or regulatory tribunal first has found that the market's structural features indicate that the pricing conduct in question is likely to injure competition (Elzinga and Mills 1989; Joskow and Klevorick 1979). The logic of the structural filter approach is that careful categorization of costs and the reconstruction of price-cost relationships is unnecessary when the market is so porous that new entrants easily can arise to attack the predator, regardless of how sharply the predator cuts its prices to subdue a specific rival. The height and durability of barriers to entry are central to the application of structural filter tests.

The third approach is the "no-rule" school. No-rule enthusiasts regard successful attempts to exclude rivals through predatory pricing to be so rare and irrational that antitrust tribunals should ignore dominant firm pricing behavior (Bork 1978, 154; Easterbrook 1981; McGee 1958, 1980). Given the infrequency with which genuinely dangerous below-cost pricing is believed to occur, no-rule adherents warn that legal constraints upon price-cutting far more often than not are likely to discourage desirable price competition. It should be noted, however, that no-rule proposals generally do not address possible efforts by regulated firms to finance predation in competitive service markets with revenues gained from services for which the regulated firm has a statutory monopoly.

The fourth approach builds heavily upon recent economic research dealing with game theory and strategic behavior. Unlike no-rule proponents, the game theoretic/strategic behavior school regards predatory pricing as a rational business strategy under certain conditions. This approach rejects the primacy of cost-price relationships and proposes the use of models involving dynamic, repeated game scenarios and asymmetric information to analyze exclusionary pricing conduct on a case-by-case basis (Jacquemin 1987, 94-137; Ordover and Saloner 1989; Phlips 1988, 197-242; Shapiro 1989; Tirole 1988, 361-88; Williamson 1989).

3.2.2. Trends in Judicial Analysis

American courts have decided over 120 reported antitrust cases involving predatory pricing allegations since the mid-1970s, when Areeda and Turner transformed academic analysis of dominant firm exclusionary pricing by introducing their cost-based predation standard (DeSanti and Kovacic 1990). As a group, these decisions have used analytical techniques that are likely to be applied by courts and postal regulatory tribunals to design tests for resolving predatory pricing claims in the postal services sector. Several features of modern American judicial decisions involving predatory pricing deserve mention.

First, American courts today generally emphasize the attainment of allocative efficiency as the appropriate basis for devising antitrust rules, including safeguards against predatory pricing (Kovacic 1990; Kovacic 1991). Decisions of the Supreme Court and the lower courts in the United States today typically analyze predation claims in terms of the likely efficiency consequences of the challenged behavior. Judicial opinions generally focus on the probability that a given strategy will enable the alleged predator to restrict output and raise prices following the demise of the target of the exclusionary pricing campaign. This is an important adjustment away from American antitrust jurisprudence of the 1960s and early 1970s, when the Supreme Court displayed an acute wariness toward dominant firm behavior (including aggressive pricing conduct) and emphasized the attainment of nonefficiency objectives, such as the preservation of opportunities for small businesses to compete.[20]

Second, the emergence of a strong efficiency orientation in the American courts in antitrust cases has been accompanied by widespread adoption of "Chicago School" analytical perspectives.[21] American courts have not endorsed the no-rule

20 See Utah Pie Co. v. Continental Baking Co., 386 U.S. 685 (1967); Brown Shoe Co. v. United States, 370 U.S. 294 (1962).

standard for predatory pricing advocated by commentators such as Bork (1978) and Easterbrook (1980), but their approach to claims of exclusionary pricing has been one of deep skepticism. In its influential decision in *Matsushita Electrical Industrial Co. v. Zenith Radio Corp.*,[22] the Supreme Court noted a "consensus among commentators that predatory pricing schemes are rarely tried and even more rarely successful" and directed courts to dismiss predatory pricing claims that lack economic "rationality."[23]

Third, courts generally have endorsed the use of price-cost relationships as the starting point for evaluating predatory pricing allegations. In developing cost-based pricing standards, courts have applied three basic presumptions: (a) pricing below average variable cost creates a rebuttable presumption of illegality; (b) pricing below average total cost but at or above average variable cost creates a rebuttable presumption of legality; and (c) pricing at or above average total cost creates a conclusive presumption of legality. In assessing the validity of pricing below average variable cost or in the range between average variable cost and average total cost, courts will entertain evidence concerning entry conditions and the existence of a reasonable business justification for the defendant's conduct—such as temporary pricing below average variable cost as part of a promotional pricing campaign to introduce a new product.

Fourth, with greater reliance upon objectively ascertainable criteria (such as price-cost relationships) to identify unlawful pricing, American courts have deemphasized the use of subjective expressions of the defendant's purpose to determine whether its pricing behavior was improper. Although there are important examples to the contrary, courts increasingly have come to disregard statements contained in documents or testimony that indicate the defendant's desire to ruin its rivals or to capture the entire market for itself.[24]

Fifth, a growing number of courts today begin the analysis of predatory pricing by asking whether the plaintiff has proven the existence of the structural preconditions for successful predation and therefore has demonstrated a likelihood that the defendant will recoup its investment in below-cost pricing.[25] Building on the

---

21 See Continental T.V., Inc. v. GTE Sylvania, Inc., 433 U.S. 36 (1977).

22 475 U.S. 574 (1986).

23 *Matsushita*, 475 U.S. at 589, 596-97.

24 See, e.g., Barry Wright Corp. v. ITT Grinnell Corp., 724 F.2d 227, 232 (1st Cir. 1983) ("'intent to harm' without more offers too vague a standard in a world where executives may think no further than 'Let's get more business,' and long-term effects on consumers depend in large measure on competitors' resources"); A.A. Poultry Farms, Inc. v. Rose Acre Farms, Inc., 881 F.2d 1396, 1400-02 (7th Cir. 1989) (statements of the defendant's subjective motivation deemed unreliable basis for applying predatory pricing safeguards), cert. denied, 494 U.S. 1019 (1990); but see Delaware & Hudson R.R. v. Consolidated Ry., 902 F.2d 174 (2d Cir.) (relying upon expressions of exclusionary purpose in defendant's documents to support finding of illegal monopolization), cert. denied, 111 S. Ct. 2041 (1990); McGahee v. Northern Propane Gas Co., 858 F.2d 1487 (11th Cir. 1988) (statements of the defendant's intent deemed relevant to analysis of predatory pricing claim), cert. denied, 490 U.S. 1084 (1989).

insights of the structural filter school, this approach usually has involved close scrutiny of entry conditions to determine whether the defendant's efforts to raise prices following exit by the plaintiff will be defeated by increased output from new entrants or expansion by fringe firms (Goldstein 1991).

In *Brooke Group, Ltd. v. Brown & Williamson, Inc.*,[26] the U.S. Supreme Court recently underscored the role of recoupment in rejecting predatory pricing allegations brought under the predatory pricing provision of the Robinson-Patman Act, which prohibits certain forms of price discrimination.[27] There Liggett & Myers alleged that Brown & Williamson (B&W) used below-cost pricing to subdue Liggett's efforts to sell generic cigarettes in competition with B&W's branded cigarettes. The Supreme Court sustained the dismissal of a $148.8 million jury verdict for Liggett, mainly because Liggett failed to show how B&W (which had a 12 percent market share) could recoup its investment in below-cost sales. The Court reached this conclusion even though high level B&W corporate documents suggested that B&W recouped its investment in predation in the generic cigarette market instantaneously by halting the erosion of its sales of branded cigarettes.[28]

The *Brooke Group* opinion said that plaintiffs alleging unlawfully low pricing under the U.S. antitrust laws must show that the "prices complained of are below an appropriate measure of its rival's costs" and must demonstrate that the defendant "had a reasonable prospect . . . of recouping its investment in below-cost pricing." The essence of recoupment is a showing that "the structure and conditions of the relevant market" would enable the alleged predator to engage in "sustained supracompetitive pricing" once its prey has been subdued. As it had done in earlier decisions such as *Matsushita*,[29] the Supreme Court declined to bar the pursuit of predatory pricing claims, but it rejected Liggett's claims and endorsed a relatively permissive standard out of fear that stronger controls on pricing conduct might render antitrust suits "a tool for keeping prices high."[30]

---

25 See A.A. Poultry Farms, Inc. v. Rose Acre Farms, Inc., 851 F.2d 1396 (7th Cir. 1989), cert. denied, 494 U.S. 1019 (1990).

26 113 S. Ct. 2578 (1993).

27 15 U.S.C. § 13(a).

28 See Burnett (1993).

29 In *Matsushita* (1986), the Supreme Court observed that "the success of any predatory scheme depends on *maintaining* that power for long enough both to recoup the predator's losses and to harvest some additional gain." 475 U.S. at 589 (emphasis in original). The Court stressed that "without barriers to entry it would presumably be impossible to maintain supracompetitive prices for an extended time." Later the same year, in reviewing a private challenge to a merger under the Clayton Act's merger control provision, the Supreme Court said that courts confronted with predatory pricing allegations "should focus on whether significant entry barriers would exist *after* the [predator] had eliminated some of its rivals, because at that point the remaining firms would begin to charge supracompetitive prices, and the barriers that existed during the competitive conditions might well prove insignificant." Cargill, Inc. v. Monfort of Colorado, Inc., 479 U.S. 104, 119-20 n.15 (1986) (emphasis in original).

30 Liggett's recoupment theory was that B&W used below-cost pricing in the generic market to force Liggett to raise its prices for generic cigarettes and to enable B&W and other sellers in

Sixth, although some decisions have suggested contrary approaches,[31] courts examining predatory pricing claims against incumbent regulated utilities generally have rejected arguments that pricing below fully distributed cost constitutes improper cross-subsidization.[32] In antitrust challenges to AT&T's pricing behavior, courts generally have concluded that the relationship of price to reasonably anticipated marginal cost (i.e., long-run incremental cost) is the proper test of predatory pricing.[33] Other recent cases involving defendants other than regulated monopolists have concluded that the appropriate focus in a predatory pricing inquiry is whether the defendant's price covers its incremental costs, not the means by which the defendant finances its price-cutting strategy.[34]

Seventh, the new industrial organization literature dealing with game theory and strategy behavior has yet to exert an influence on judicial analysis of predatory pricing claims (Klevorick 1993). However, previous experience with the judiciary's application of economics in deciding antitrust cases in the United States shows that there is a lag of roughly ten to fifteen years between the time ideas first appear in economics journals until they find their way into the citations of court opinions

---

the highly concentrated cigarette industry to stabilize prices at higher levels. Through tacit oligopolistic coordination, industry members then would sustain generic prices at supracompetitive levels. Recoupment would occur mainly by severely reducing the "cannibalization" (by low-cost generic cigarettes) of sales of branded cigarettes. To the Supreme Court, the tacit coordination scenario was theoretically plausible, but it lacked a sufficient evidentiary basis to permit a jury to infer that B&W's conduct posed "an authentic threat to competition." The Court emphasized that relying on tacit coordination by oligopolists to achieve recoupment is highly speculative, given the difficulties that oligopolists face in orchestrating their behavior at arms length.

31 See United States v. Western Electric Co., 1991-2 Trade Cas. (CCH) ¶ 69,503 (D.D.C. 1991).

32 For example, in *Northeastern Telephone*, the U.S. Court of Appeals for the Second Circuit observed that the plaintiff's "argument in favor of the fully distributed cost test is based on a misunderstanding of the economic notion of subsidization." 651 F.2d at 90. The court went on to explain:

Northeastern seems to believe that whenever a product's price fails to cover fully distributed costs, the enterprise must subsidize that product's revenues with revenues earned elsewhere. But when the price of an item exceeds its costs directly attributable to its production, that is, when price exceeds marginal or average variable cost, no subsidy is necessary. On the contrary, any surplus can be used to defray the firm's non-allocable expenses.

33 See *MCI*, 708 F.2d at 1114, 1119-23 (rejecting predatory pricing claim against AT&T where AT&T's prices for certain telephone services remained at or above long-run incremental cost); *Northeastern Telephone*, 651 F.2d at 90 (rejecting application of a fully distributed cost standard and endorsing the use of a long-run incremental cost test).

34 See Clamp-All Corp. v. Cast Iron Soil Pipe Institute, 851 F.2d 478 (1st Cir. 1988), cert. denied, 488 U.S. 1007 (1989). Judge Stephen Breyer's opinion in *Clamp-All* observed that "[i]f the [defendant's] price is unlawfully low, if, for example, it is a predatory price, it does not ordinarily matter whether the money to pay for the resulting temporary loss comes from a bank account, a legacy, a lottery prize, or the proceeds of a price-fixing conspiracy in respect to another product; regardless of the financing source, the practice would be unlawful." 851 F.2d at 485-86. Judge Breyer added "We do not see how a dubious kind of 'financing source' could, in and of itself, convert a lawful low price into an unlawful one." Id. at 486.

(Kovacic 1992b). Although the game theoretic and strategic behavior literature poses formidable administrability challenges to judges seeking to devise operational legal standards, it is likely to be only a matter of time before courts begin applying principles first articulated by economists in the late 1970s and early 1980s.[35] The U.S. Supreme Court's 1992 decision in *Image Technical Services, Inc. v. Eastman Kodak Co.*[36] made extensive use of the "post-Chicago" literature dealing with information theory in refusing to dismiss tying-related antitrust claims against Kodak (Lande 1993).

Compared to the recent experience of American courts in addressing allegations of predatory pricing under the antitrust laws, the European Commission has adjudicated many fewer predatory pricing cases under Article 86 of the Treaty of Rome. Thus, Commission jurisprudence applying the Article 86 prohibition against the abuse of a dominant position to price-cutting is less well-developed. Nonetheless, one can identify some important differences between the legal regimes in the EC and the United States (Adams 1985; Waller 1992). In general terms, these differences indicate that the Commission will scrutinize predatory pricing allegations more closely and will give dominant firms less discretion to set price levels under Article 86 than United States courts currently afford dominant firms under the Sherman Act.

The Commission's approach to addressing predatory pricing claims under Article 86 departs from American practice in three major respects. The first deals with goals that the Commission seeks to effectuate in applying Article 86. The Commission has not embraced the singleminded focus of many American courts on economic efficiency. Instead, Commission decisions dealing with dominant firm behavior continue to give effect to non-efficiency values, such as the protection of competitors and the maintenance of a more egalitarian business environment.[37] The greater solicitude for smaller firms as an independent aim of competition policy will incline the Commission more often to constrain dominant firm pricing discretion where price-cutting threatens to eliminate (or has extinguished) a smaller rival.

Second, the Commission tends to define relevant markets more narrowly than American courts. This increases the likelihood that the defendant will be found to possess a large share of commercial activity in the market in question. Commission decisions often find the condition of "dominance" to be satisfied at market share thresholds considerably lower than American courts ordinarily would apply in

---

35 The rate at which post-Chicago insights are absorbed into the judicial mainstream likely will be retarded by the relatively narrow antitrust preferences of judges chosen by Presidents Ronald Reagan and George Bush, who together appointed about two-thirds of the current federal judiciary. See Kovacic (1991; 1993).

36 112 S. Ct. 2072 (1992).

37 For example, Hawk (1990, 11, 13) notes the "EEC's greater willingness to introduce social and political values directly into antitrust analysis" and concludes that "the EEC has largely resisted the Chicago School approach which underlies much of the U.S. antitrust revolution." See also Fox (1986).

determining whether the defendant has substantial market power in a Sherman Act dispute. EC tribunals have found dominance with market shares as low as 40 to 45 percent where the shares of the dominant firm's rivals are much smaller and other factors (such as technological superiority) suggest the ability to exercise market control (American Bar Association, 1992, 951-53). By contrast, in Sherman Act jurisprudence, the threshold of concern usually is 65 percent in a monopolization case and 50 percent in an attempted monopolization case. Thus, large firms stand a greater chance of being deemed "dominant" for Article 86 purposes than they do of being found to have market power for Sherman Act Section 2 purposes (Waller 1992, 68-69).

Third, Commission predatory pricing standards generally pose greater dangers for large firms that engage in aggressive pricing behavior. The Commission considers price-cost comparisons, but it has declined to articulate price-cost tests with the clarity (and predictability) of American antitrust courts. Nor do static price-cost standards play as large a role in Commission analysis; rather, the Commission gives heavier emphasis to documentary or testimonial evidence of the defendant's intent in evaluating the legality of challenged pricing conduct. In future predation disputes, the Commission is likely to be receptive to strategic behavior models offered by post-Chicago commentators (Hawk 1990, 13).

The 1991 decision of the European Court of Justice in *Akzo Chemie BV v. European Commission*[38] illustrates the distinctive nature of judicial analysis of predatory pricing under Article 86. In *Akzo* the Court upheld a Commission finding that the defendant producer of industrial chemicals have violated Article 86 by using predatory pricing to discipline a smaller rival.[39] The defendant's 50 percent share of a relevant market was deemed sufficient to establish the requisite condition of dominance.[40] The Court ruled that the defendant had abused its dominant position by pricing some products below average variable cost and pricing others below average total cost with an intent to eliminate its rival. *Akzo* indicates that EC competition tribunals will attach lesser weight to cost-based tests and will pay closer attention to evidence revealing the defendant's subjective motive (Hawk 1990, 882-85).

3.3. Denials of Access to Essential Facilities

The efforts of firms to provide services previously offered only by a regulated monopolist frequently raise questions about the ability of entrants to gain access to networks or assets over which the regulated incumbent still retains exclusive

38 62/86 (July 3, 1991); see also "Court Confirms Commission's Approach on Predatory Pricing," *Common Market Reports* (CCH) No. 686 (July 25, 1991).

39 See O. J. L 374/1 (Dec. 31, 1985), *Common Market Reporter* (CCH) ¶ 10,748.

40 As noted above, American courts applying Section 2 of the Sherman Act generally decline to find monopoly power unless the defendant holds a market share of 65 percent or higher in a properly defined relevant market. See American Bar Association (1992, 212-14).

control (Tye 1987). Recent experience with competition in the American electric power and telecommunications industries illustrates the phenomenon. Competition in the electric utility industry has generated numerous disputes concerning requests by unintegrated local distribution systems for access to the transmission facilities of integrated utilities. In the telecommunications industry, access issues today figure prominently in challenges to the policies of regulated local exchange carriers concerning interconnection to the carriers' local networks and the co-location of an entrant's equipment inside the facilities of the local exchange carriers.

Antitrust litigation has provided an important avenue for entrants to press demands for access. In American antitrust cases, these efforts have spurred the development of the "essential facility doctrine." This principle bars a monopolist's refusal to allow access to a facility whose availability is vital to the competitive capability of rivals in upstream or downstream markets (Kovacic 1992a). The foundational cases presenting essential facility claims have involved regulated utilities,[41] and the doctrine supplies an analytical framework that regulatory commissions and antitrust authorities are likely to apply or adapt in considering access disputes involving postal monopolies.

As developed by American antitrust courts, the essential facility doctrine has five basic components: (1) a monopolist controls the facility in question, (2) it is commercially impractical or unreasonable for the monopolist's competitors to duplicate the facility, (3) the monopolist has denied the use of the facility to its rival, or has offered access only on unreasonable terms, (4) providing access on the entrant's preferred terms must be technically and economically feasible, and (5) no plausible business justification supports the monopolist's denial or restriction of access.[42]

Most commentators regard the essential facility doctrine with apprehension (Baker 1993; Areeda and Hovenkamp 1992; Werden 1984). The doctrine's greatest perceived danger is that courts and regulators will freely attach the label of "essential" to any asset that confers a competitive advantage upon its owner and will proceed to compel access. Forcing access to broadly defined categories of essential facilities may seriously reduce incentives to create, maintain, and improve such assets.

These criteria raise three basic economic and regulatory policy issues. The first concerns the proper definition of what is "essential" (Larson et al. 1994). Recent judicial decisions have emphasized that it is not enough for the plaintiff to argue that the defendant's conduct imposed a cost disadvantage or reduced the plaintiff's

41 See, e.g., United States v. Otter Tail Power Co., 410 U.S. 366 (1973) (monopolization claim involving refusal by integrated utility to "wheel" power over its transmission lines for the use of a non-integrated local distribution company); *MCI*, 708 F.2d at 1132 (monopolization claim involving refusal by AT&T to provide interconnection arrangements for rival supplier of long distance telephone services).

42 These criteria are derived mainly from two recent antitrust decisions. See Aspen Skiing Co. v. Aspen Highlands Skiing Corp., 472 U.S. 585, 605 (1985); *MCI*, 708 F.2d at 1132-33.

profits. To show that a facility is "essential," the plaintiff "must show something more than inconvenience, or even some economic loss; he must show that an alternative to the facility is not feasible."[43] In applying the essentiality screen to claims involving regulated industries, courts have tended to proceed from a rebuttable presumption that assets such as pipelines, transmission lines, and local distribution networks are essential facilities. As a rough operating hypothesis, such a presumption may be reasonable, given the frequency with which such assets display natural monopoly traits. The appropriateness of this presumption in practice, however, depends crucially upon how readily courts and regulatory bodies will allow the defendant/owner of the contested asset to rebut the presumption.

The second critical policy issue concerns the justifications that courts and regulators will accept as bases for the regulated monopolist to deny access outright, or to impose conditions or access fees that the entrant deems unreasonable. Among the chief hazards attending the application of the essential facility doctrine is the possibility that judges and regulators will assume too readily that access can be ordered without damaging the facility or otherwise undermining incentives for good performance by the regulated monopolist. Antitrust courts long have allowed the regulated monopolist to curtail or condition access on the ground that acceding to the entrant's demands might impede the proper functioning of the facility.[44] Recent decisions have expanded the regulated firm's ability to justify its conduct by reference to conditions and constraints imposed by the operation of the regulatory regime under which it operates.[45] Thus, where regulation compels the regulated monopolist to achieve wealth distribution objectives or other ends unrelated to efficiency, the monopolist may be able to argue successfully that its denial or

---

43 Twin Laboratories, Inc. v. Weider Health & Fitness, 900 F.2d 566, 570 (2d Cir. 1990); see also City of Chanute v. Williams Natural Gas Co., 955 F.2d 641, 649 (10th Cir. 1992) (denial of essential facility must result in a "severe handicap" to the plaintiff); Alaska Airlines, Inc. v. United Airlines, Inc., 948 F.2d 536, 544 (9th Cir. 1992) ("A facility that is controlled by a single firm will be considered 'essential' only if control of the facility carries with it the power to *eliminate* competition in the downstream market" [emphasis in original]).

44 See, e.g., City of Groton v. Connecticut Light & Power Co., 662 F.2d 921 (2d Cir. 1981) (sustaining electric utility's refusal to wheel power where the plaintiff failed to specify the quantity of power to be wheeled or the timing of the transaction); Town of Massena v. Niagara Mohawk Power Co., 1980-2 Trade Cas. (CCH) ¶ 63,526 (N.D.N.Y. 1980) (refusing to compel access to transmission facilities where the entrant failed to resolve legitimate engineering concerns).

45 See, e.g., City of Anaheim v. Southern California Edison Co., 955 F.2d 1373, 1381 (9th Cir. 1992) (refusing to impose duty on integrated electric utility to devote transmission capacity to serve a municipal distribution company's wheeling requirements where complying with the request would serve mainly to shift costs from one set of the integrated utility's customers to another); Phonetele Co. v. AT&T Co., 664 F.2d 716, 737-38 (9th Cir. 1981) ("if a defendant can establish that, at the time the various anticompetitive acts alleged here were taken, it had a reasonable basis to conclude that its actions were necessitated by concrete factual imperatives recognized as legitimate by the regulatory authority, then its actions did not violate the antitrust laws").

conditioning of access was justified by its good faith efforts to fulfill regulatory commands (Tye 1991, 414-16).

When a court or regulatory commission decides to compel access to the monopolist's facilities, it must address a third major policy issue: on what terms and at what price shall access be provided? If a reviewing authority requires a monopolist to provide access, it must be prepared to tell the monopolist how much it may charge the entrant (Baumol and Sidak 1994; Tye 1993). Addressing the question of appropriate access terms and fees also raises the choice of institutions for setting access conditions.

Experience with essential facility claims in antitrust litigation in the United States suggests that courts are institutionally ill-suited to perform regulatory functions such as ratemaking. The desirability of applying an essential facility doctrine is directly related to the adequacy of remedial tools at the court's disposal to set access terms. As Areeda and Turner (1978, 241) observe, "requiring a vertically integrated monopolist to deal with outsiders requires some mechanism for supervising and adjusting the price and other terms of dealing. No such mechanism ordinarily is available to the antitrust court." Such considerations may warrant placing responsibility for determining whether access is required and for setting access prices within a regulatory commission (rather than delegating such responsibility to an antitrust court), with the decisions of regulatory officials being subject to judicial review.

Compared to American antitrust courts, the European Commission and Court of Justice generally have treated dominant firm refusals to deal less tolerantly and have shown a stronger inclination to compel such entities to give rival service providers access to bottleneck facilities (Hawk 1990, 855). Early Commission and Court of Justice decisions that addressed refusal to deal allegations focused almost exclusively upon "fairness" considerations, slighted efficiency effects, and generally displayed extreme suspicion of dominant firm refusals to cooperate with rivals. More recent actions by these tribunals have moderated these tendencies, but EC competition jurisprudence still displays a greater willingness to regulate dominant firm conduct. As Kauper (1991, 455) explains, "the willingness of the Commission and Court to mandate continued dealing, displace private decision-making, and take on the obligation to supervise the terms of dealing, which is inherent in requiring firms to deal, far exceeds the willingness of American courts to do the same."

Several EC decisions have applied refusal to deal concepts to regulated firms such as telecommunications companies and postal authorities. In *British Telecommunications*,[46] the Commission found that British Telecom had violated Article 86 by abusing its dominant position as the holder of a statutory monopoly to provide telecommunications services within the United Kingdom. British Telecom's unlawful conduct consisted of refusing to allow private message-forwarding firms in

---

46 O. J. L 360/36 (Dec. 21, 1982), *Common Market Reporter* (CCH) ¶ 10,443.

the United Kingdom to relay telex messages that had been received from and were intended for other countries. The Commission emphasized that the telephone monopolist's refusal to deal impeded the ability of users in other EC member states to take advantage of differences in tariff structures or real costs. More recently, the Commission has used refusal to deal theories under Article 86 to challenge efforts by French and German postal authorities to prevent entry into new markets or to extend their regulated monopoly into new markets.[47] Subsequent Commission announcements have indicated a continuing interest in challenging efforts by regulated firms to obstruct new entry.

4. Conclusion

The deregulation of the postal services sector will confront policymakers with problems similar to issues that courts and regulatory bodies have addressed previously in dealing with the introduction of competition in other regulated industries. These experiences suggest that we can expect a growing volume of disputes concerning pricing and network access policies adopted by postal service monopolists in response to new entry. Analytical models developed through antitrust adjudication by EC and United States antitrust tribunals will influence the development of standards governing responses of incumbent postal firms to entry.

In the area of pricing conduct, the jurisprudence of American and EC courts, respectively, provides notably different approaches for controlling dominant firm conduct. American antitrust courts have adopted a strong efficiency orientation in Sherman Act litigation and have relied heavily on permissive cost-based standards to give dominant firms broad freedom to respond to entry. In examining regulated firm behavior, American courts have tended to dismiss concerns about cross-subsidization so long as the defendant can show that its prices recovered its long-run incremental costs. The European Commission, by contrast, has placed greater emphasis on the preservation of opportunities for smaller firms to compete and has relied extensively upon evidence other than the defendant's price-cost relationships to determine liability under Article 86 of the Treaty of Rome. EC antitrust thinking currently is more hospitable to the adoption of post-Chicago economic analysis that emphasizes strategic behavior.

Antitrust case law and commentary also supply an important frame of reference for resolving disputes concerning access to the assets (such as local distribution networks) of postal service monopolists. Here also EC and United States antitrust approaches diverge, with the Commission showing a greater inclination to compel dominant firms to grant access to essential facilities or otherwise cooperate with rivals. The wisdom of requiring access under the EC or United States competition policy regimes will depend upon how carefully "essential" assets are identified,

---

47 See Krause (1986); 48 *Antitrust and Trade Regulation Reports* (BNA) 410 (Feb. 28, 1985).

justifications for access restrictions are analyzed, and rates for access are set.

References

Adams, Gregory B. 1985. "European and American Antitrust Regulation of Pricing by Monopolists." *Vanderbilt Journal of Transnational Law* 18: 1-70.

American Bar Association. 1992. *Antitrust Law Developments (Third Edition)*. Chicago: American Bar Association.

Areeda, Philip, and Herbert Hovenkamp. 1993. *Antitrust Law: Supplement*. Boston: Little, Brown.

Areeda, Philip, and Donald Turner. 1978. *Antitrust Law* (Vol. III). Boston: Little, Brown.

Areeda, Philip, and Donald Turner. 1975. "Predatory Pricing and Related Practices Under Section 2 of the Sherman Act." *Harvard Law Review* 88: 697-733.

Baker, Donald I. 1994. "Compulsory Access to Network Joint Ventures Under the Sherman Act: Rules or Roulette? *Utah Law Review* 1993: 999-1133.

Baumol, William J., and J. Gregory Sidak. 1994. *Toward Competition in Local Telephony*. Washington, D.C.: American Enterprise Institute.

Baumol, William J., and J. Gregory Sidak. 1994. "Pricing of Inputs Sold to Competitors." *Yale Journal on Regulation* 11: 171-202.

Bork, Robert H. 1978. *The Antitrust Paradox*. New York: Basic Books.

Burnett, William B. 1993. "Predation by a Nondominant Firm: The Liggett Case." In *The Antitrust Revolution*, edited by John E. Kwoka, Jr. and Lawrence J. White. Glenview, Illinois: Scott, Forsman.

Campbell, Jr., James I. 1993. "The Postal Green Paper Debate in the European Community." Mimeo.

Campbell, Jr., James I. 1992. "The Future of the Universal Postal Union." In *Regulation and the Nature of Postal and Delivery Services*, edited by Michael A. Crew and Paul R. Kleindorfer. Boston: Kluwer Academic Publishers.

Commission of the European Community. 1992. *Green Paper on the Development of the Single Market for Postal Services* ["EC Green Paper"]. Luxembourg: Office for Official Publications of the European Community.

Craig, Roger P., and William T. Alvis. 1977. "The Postal Monopoly: Two Hundred Years of Covering Commercial as Well as Personal Messages." *University of San Francisco Law Review* 12: 57-87.

Crew, Michael A., and Paul R. Kleindorfer. 1992. *The Economics of Postal Service*. Boston: Kluwer Academic Publishers.

DeSanti, Susan S., and William E. Kovacic. 1990. "*Matsushita*: Its Construction and Application by the Lower Courts." *Antitrust Law Journal* 59: 609-53.

Dobbenberg, Philip. 1992. "The International Mail Market in the1990s." In *Regulation and the Nature of Postal and Delivery Services*, edited by Michael A. Crew and Paul R. Kleindorfer. Boston: Kluwer Academic Publishers.

Dobbs, Ian, and Paul Richards. 1992. "Policy Implications of Postal Network Access." In *Regulation and the Nature of Postal and Delivery Services*, edited by Michael A. Crew and Paul R. Kleindorfer. Boston: Kluwer Academic Publishers.

Easterbrook, Frank H. 1981. "Predatory Strategies and Counterstrategies." *University of Chicago Law Review* 48: 263-337.

Elzinga, Kenneth G., and Alan Mills. 1989. "Testing for Predation: Is Recoupment Feasible." *Antitrust Bulletin* 34: 869-93.

Fox, Eleanor M. 1986. "Monopolization and Dominance in the United States and the

European Community: Efficiency, Opportunity, and Fairness." *Notre Dame Law Review* 61: 981-1020.

Goldstein, Jessica L. 1991. "Single Firm Predatory Pricing in Antitrust Law: The *Rose Acre* Recoupment Test and the Search for an Appropriate Judicial Standard." *Columbia Law Review* 91: 1757-92.

Hawk, Barry E. 1990. II *United States, Common Market and International Antitrust: A Comparative Guide*. New York: Prentice Hall.

Hurwitz, James D., and William E. Kovacic. 1983. "Judicial Analysis of Predation: The Emerging Trends." *Vanderbilt Law Review* 35: 63-157.

Joskow, Paul L., and Alvin Klevorick K. 1979. "A Framework for Analyzing Predatory Pricing Policy." *Yale Law Journal* 89: 213-70.

Kahn, Alfred E. 1992. "Market Power Issues in Deregulated Industries." *Antitrust Law Journal* 60: 857-66.

Kauper, Thomas E. 1991. "Article 86, Excessive Prices, and Refusals to Deal." *Antitrust Law Journal* 59: 441-56.

Klevorick, Alvin K. 1993. "The Current State of the Law and Economics of Predatory Pricing." *American Economic Review* 83: 162-67.

Kovacic, William E. 1993. "Judicial Appointments and the Future of Antitrust Policy." *Antitrust* 7(2): 8-13.

Kovacic, William E. 1992a. "The Antitrust Law and Economics of Essential Facilities in Public Utility Regulation." In *Economic Innovations in Public Utility Regulation*, edited by Michael A. Crew. Boston: Kluwer Academic Publishers.

Kovacic, William E. 1992b. "The Influence of Economics On Antitrust Law." *Economic Inquiry* 30: 294-306.

Kovacic, William E. 1991. "Reagan's Judicial Appointees and Antitrust in the 1990s." *Fordham Law Review* 60: 49-124.

Kovacic, William E. 1990. "*The Antitrust Paradox* Revisited: Robert Bork and the Transformation of Modern Antitrust Policy." *Wayne Law Review* 36: 1413-71.

Krause, Barbara L. 1986. "Private International Couriers: A Challenge to the West Germany Postal Monopoly and EEC Law." *Cornell International Law Journal* 19: 35-63.

Lande, Robert H. 1993. "Chicago Takes It on the Chin: Imperfect Information Could Play a Crucial Role in the Post-*Kodak* World." *Antitrust Law Journal* 62: 193-202.

Larson, Alexander C., William E. Kovacic, and Douglas R. Mudd. 1994 (forthcoming). "Competitive Access Issues and Telecommunications Regulatory Policy." *Journal of Contemporary Law* 20.

Larson, Alexander C., and William E. Kovacic. 1990. "Predatory Pricing Safeguards in Telecommunications Regulation: Removing Impediments to Competition." *St. Louis University Law Journal* 35: 1-38.

McGee, John. 1980. "Predatory Pricing Revisited." *Journal of Law and Economics* 23: 289-330.

McGee, John. 1958. "Predatory Price Cutting: The Standard Oil (N.J.) Case." *Journal of Law and Economics* 1: 137-69.

Ordover, Janusz A., and Garth Saloner. 1989. "Predation, Monopolization, and Antitrust." In I *Handbook of Industrial Organization*, edited by Richard Schmalensee & Robert D. Willig. Amsterdam: North Holland.

Organization for Economic Cooperation and Development, Committee on Competition Law and Policy ["OECD"]. 1988. *Predatory Pricing*. Paris: Organization for Economic Cooperation and Development.

Owen, Bruce M., and Robert D. Willig. 1983. "Economics and Postal Pricing." In *The Future of the Postal Service*, edited by Joel Fleischmann. Aspen: Aspen Institute.

Panzar, John. 1991. "Is Postal Service a Natural Monopoly?" In *Competition and Innovation in Postal Services*, edited by Michael A. Crew and Paul R. Kleindorfer. Boston: Kluwer Academic Publishers.

Panzar, John. 1992. "Competition, Efficiency and the Vertical Structure of Postal Services." In *Regulation and the Nature of Postal and Delivery Services*, edited by Michael A. Crew and Paul R. Kleindorfer. Boston: Kluwer Academic Publishers.

Phlips, Louis. 1988. *The Economics of Imperfect Information.* Cambridge: Cambridge University Press.

Priest, George. 1975. "The History of the Postal Monopoly in the United States." *Journal of Law and Economics* 18: 33-80.

Rogerson, Cathy M., and William M. Takis. 1992. "Economies of Scale and Scope and Competition in Postal Services." In *Regulation and the Nature of Postal and Delivery Services*, edited by Michael A. Crew and Paul R. Kleindorfer. Boston: Kluwer Academic Publishers.

Shapiro, Carl. 1989. "The Theory of Business Strategy." *RAND Journal of Economics* 20: 125-37.

Sherman, Roger. 1991. "Competition in Postal Service." In *Competition and Innovation in Postal Services*, edited by Michael A. Crew and Paul R. Kleindorfer. Boston: Kluwer Academic Publishers.

Sievers, Mark, and Brooks Albery. 1992. "Strategic Allocation of Overhead: The Application of Traditional Predation Tests to Multiproduct Firms." *Antitrust Law Journal* 60: 757-84.

Stumpf, Ulrich. 1992. "Remailing in the European Community: Economic Analysis of Alternative Regulatory Environments." In *Regulation and the Nature of Postal and Delivery Services*, edited by Michael A. Crew and Paul R. Kleindorfer. Boston: Kluwer Academic Publishers.

Stumpf, Ulrich. 1991. "Postal Newspaper Delivery and Diversity of Opinions." In *Competition and Innovation in Postal Services*, edited by Michael A. Crew and Paul R. Kleindorfer. Boston: Kluwer Academic Publishers.

Sullivan, Lawrence A. 1977. *Antitrust.* Minneapolis: West Publishing Co.

Temin, Peter. 1987. *The Fall of the Bell System.* Cambridge: Cambridge University Press.

Tirole, Jean. 1988. *The Theory of Industrial Organization.* Cambridge, MA: MIT Press.

Tye, William B. 1993. "Pricing Market Access for Regulated Firms." *Logistics and Transportation Review* 29: 39-67.

Tye, William B. 1991. *The Transition to Deregulation—Developing Economic Standards for Public Policies.* New York: Quorum Books.

Tye, William B. 1987. "Competitive Access: A Comparative Industry Approach to the Essential Facility Doctrine." *Energy Law Journal* 8: 337-79.

Waller, Spencer Weber. 1992. "Understanding and Appreciating EC Competition Law." *Antitrust Law Journal* 61: 55-77.

Werden, Gregory. 1984. "The Law and Economics of the Essential Facility Doctrine." *St. Louis University Law Journal* 32: 433-80.

Williamson, Oliver E. 1987. "Delimiting Antitrust." *Georgetown Law Journal* 76: 271-303.